* Volumes with an asterisk following the title are a part of the NCRLL set: Approaches to Language and Literacy Research, edited by JoBeth Allen and Donna Alvermann.

(Continued)

New Literacies in Action
Teaching and Learning in Multiple Media

William Kist

Foreword by David Bloome

Teachers College, Columbia University
New York and London

Published by Teachers College Press, 1234 Amsterdam Avenue, New York, NY 10027

Library of Congress Cataloging-in-Publication Data

Kist, William
New literacies in action: teaching and learning in multiple media / William Kist; foreword by David Bloome.
  p. cm. — (Language and literacy series)
  Includes bibliographical references and index.
  ISBN 0-8077-4541-3 (cloth)—ISBN 0-8077-4540-5 (pbk.)
  1. Literacy—Social aspects—United States. 2. Media literacy—Study and teaching—United States. 3. Mass media and education—United States. I. Title. II. Language and literacy series (New York, N.Y.)

LC151.K58 2004
302.2'244—dc22   2004055309

ISBN 0-8077-4540-5 (paper)
ISBN 0-8077-4541-3 (cloth)

Printed on acid-free paper

Manufactured in the United States of America
12 11 10 09 08 07 06 05   8 7 6 5 4 3 2 1

For my parents,
Richard Clark Kist and Dorothy Levering Kist,
who filled my growing-up years with many literacies

CONTENTS

FOREWORD

At the beginning of *Call Me Ishmael*, poet Charles Olson writes: "I take SPACE to be the central fact to man born in America, from Folsom cave to now. I spell it large because it comes large here. Large, and without mercy" (p. 11). *Call Me Ishmael* is Olson's study of Herman Melville's writing of *Moby Dick*, perhaps the essential capturing of America's obsession with seeking and conquering space. I also take space to be the central fact of American life but where Melville and Olson saw space in oceans, plains, and mountains, I see space in our daily lives, in our interactions with each other, and in our classrooms.

For the time being, the New Literacies—as William Kist calls them, sophisticated uses of technology and multimodal, multigenre composition—have provided a way for some teachers and students to create new spaces for accomplishing their daily lives: for exploring the worlds in which they live, for constructing caring relationships with each other, for creating meaning, and for voicing their lives. Traveling across the United States and Canada, Kist visited teachers and students in a broad range of classrooms and localities to see how they use the New Literacies to create spaces for themselves. Describing one of his observations, Kist writes, "The child looks up . . . sets aside his worksheet, and takes out a fresh, clean piece of paper. " Exactly so.

There is no one way to fill up the space on that blank sheet of paper, no one way to do the New Literacies. In each of the classrooms described by Kist, teachers and students sat aside the worksheets and the worksheet mentality and created their own spaces, taking account of their own particular local circumstances.

Yet, despite the celebration we might have in what these teachers and students have accomplished, there is a sense of fragility in Kist's description of these classrooms. He writes, "Can a teacher really do 'new literacies' at school without its becoming a 'dominant literacy'. . . . Will 'new literacies' in a school environment become just another dominant literacy practice?" Possibly. In some of the classrooms, the students failed to move beyond the excitement of having a space for their own voices; they failed to understand the impact of media manipulation and branding. But in other cases, the students eschewed the mechanisms schools often use to control space— grades, standards, tests, and transformation of student work into hierarchical assessments of ability—and used the space created by alignment with the New Literacies to enhance their local communities. Schooling was pushed into the background, learning and responsibility toward others into the foreground.

As I see it, there is an ongoing battle over space: who owns it, who can occupy it, and who can do what, where, and with what authority and control. As some spaces close down and come under control of dominant social institutions with their assessments, standards, labeling, and worksheets, other spaces are opened. And this, perhaps, is the underlying set of stories that Kist is telling. As one of the teachers Kist interviewed noted, "Everybody draws; everybody sings."

David Bloome

REFERENCE

Olson, C. (1947). *Call me Ishmael.* San Francisco: City Lights Books.

ACKNOWLEDGMENTS

This study, which has spanned almost 7 years, would not have been possible without the help of many people and organizations. When I first began my doctoral studies, I was encouraged by several people to follow this line of research, given my interest in nonprint media: fellow doctoral students Gay Fawcett and Betsy Pryor and Professor Bev Shaklee (now of George Mason University) were all instrumental in pointing me down this path at the very beginning. My dissertation advisor, mentor, and friend, Nancy Padak, Distinguished Professor of Education at Kent State University, was behind me from the start, handing me her copy of John-Steiner's *Notebooks of the Mind* during one of our first meetings. In addition, Nancy nominated the Parma High School teachers profiled in Chapter 2. Her generosity of spirit continues to be an inspiration to so many of us whom she has mentored.

The Research Center for Educational Technology (www.rcet.org) that was later headed, in succession, by Gay Fawcett and Betsy Pryor, was responsible, along with AT&T, for the funding that supported my travel to the locations represented in this book. Gay and Betsy were completely supportive of all the twists and turns in my research. Thanks also go to my Kent State colleagues Rich Vacca, Harry Noden, Joanne Arhar, and Linda Rogers (now of University of California-Monterey Bay) as well as Hal Foster, of the University of Akron, and Jeff Wilhelm now of Boise State University, who also read early versions of some chapters and encouraged me greatly. Many thanks go as well to my Kent State colleagues Nancy McCracken and David Bruce who introduced me to David Bloome, who so eloquently wrote the foreword to this book.

My work also got a needed boost from my sister-in-law, Jo Ann Kist, who helped me transcribe the many tapes from my classroom visits; in addition, her assistance as an art history researcher was a great help.

I would not have met some of the teachers profiled in this book had it not been for the late Ann Watts Pailliotet who, when she heard of my work, immediately offered to post a nomination call in the

New Literacies section of *ReadingOnline*. I'm sorry that Ann isn't here to see the publication of this book.

Of course, all of the teachers and students profiled herein are praiseworthy. Not only have they attempted some fairly rare feats of teaching, they have permitted me to observe and write about them. I thank them for their courage and for their honesty.

I must thank Alan Luke and John Elkins, who published two of my pieces in the *Journal of Adolescent and Adult Literacy*, which gave me a needed boost of confidence. Their criticisms and editorial opinions also strengthened my work and my focus.

Sincere thanks also to Carol Collins and the editorial staff at Teachers College Press for helping make this the best book I could produce.

Many thanks to photographers Jim Martin and Scott Earhart of Studio Martone, as well as to my great friends Dennis O'Connell and Holly Barkdoll of Magical Theatre Company who introduced me to young actors Mark Leach and Greg Stalder, who posed for the cover. I am also grateful to my former school district, the Akron Public Schools, which arranged for us to do the phot shoot at Central-Hower High School.

I am also thankful to my students from the Akron Public Schools and Kent State–Stark, and colleagues from the Medina County Schools' Educational Service Center who helped me—and continue to help me—think about new literacies and further refine my thinking.

Finally, along with my sister, Nancy, and my brother, Joseph, I was lucky enough to grow up in a home with parents who surrounded us with many literacies. To them, I will always be grateful.

Chapter 1

FROM POLYTYCHS TO INSTANT
MESSAGES AND BACK AGAIN

The evening that I saw Woody Allen's *Manhattan* (Allen, 1979) was significant for me. For the first time, as a teenager, I realized that a person could "speak" through the writing and direction of a film, using camera placement, lighting, and the direction of actors to communicate directly with an audience. Until that moment, I had seen films as primarily entertainment vehicles; essentially, opportunities for performers to show off and make people laugh or cry in response to their individual performances. It didn't occur to me that a single human being could make a personal statement using this complex medium. "Before that," as I wrote several years ago,

> I had thought of film primarily as an entertainment medium, something made on a Hollywood assembly line. Now I saw that it could be a personal statement from one person. And it had its own force—I realized that I could not adequately put into words the message that [Woody] Allen was communicating by having his character fly down the street underscored by Gershwin. His communication to me could possibly be "translated" into words—something like "love is worth holding onto no matter what"—but these words couldn't begin to evoke the same understandings I received from the statement he had communicated via the filming of this character's running through the streets. (Kist, 2000, p. 710)

That a person could communicate through an art form in this way fascinated me then and still fascinates me today. So I am confessing right up front that my interest in new literacies has been prompted by my own wonderment at these highly individualized unique "statements" made by artists via media that are nonprint and nonverbal in nature. Through moving pictures, still photography, dance, theatre, music, and visual art a person can "speak" just as

1

directly and individually as through the medium of print.

My interest intensified as I became a classroom teacher and saw the power unleashed when I allowed my students to compose using non-print-based media. Although my *Manhattan* experience had taken place out of school, and I went on to make my own films, videos, and music, I also went on to become a middle school and high school English teacher and discovered the power of these new literacies in classrooms.

I quickly noticed that I would get a very strong reaction when I showed a silent film in class—Charlie Chaplin's film *The Kid* (1921), for example—and we would talk about conveying emotion and plot without words. Students were moved when viewing this silent film, the first some of them had ever seen. I would also get fantastic work when I would assign students to create their own video versions of Chaucer's *Canterbury Tales* or music video adaptations of the stories of Edgar Allen Poe. One year, I assigned each of my five ninth-grade English classes one act of Shakespeare's *Midsummer Night's Dream* to act out (with the assignment being that each student had to memorize at least two lines from the play). When we were finished, we had a video that contained the highlights of the entire play as performed by over 100 students. Students were mesmerized the day that I played the entire video to all five classes.

Of course, I was still bound to print at that point. Everything I did was tied to the printed word and making sure that students "got" what we were reading. Still, there was no escaping the power of these *new literacies*, although I certainly did not know that term at the time.

NEW LITERACIES AND ADOLESCENT USES OF MEDIA

As I became familiar with the new literacies research and writings, I soon discovered that scholars have become focused on students' uses of the media and the great differences between media experiences of students 25 years ago and students today. While I was focusing on what was on the screen and what it meant for me as an artist and as a teacher that film directors could make strong nonverbal statements, many of my colleagues have been looking out in the audience and realizing that the boundaries have blurred between Woody Allen, his audience, their identities, and even multinational entertainment companies.

For example, when my friends and I went to the movie that night

25 years ago, we organized our meeting there via telephone and face-to-face communication. We did not have email at that time, or pagers or cell phones—indeed, there was no warning at the beginning of the film asking us to turn off our cell phones. We viewed the film at the Summit Mall Cinema, which has since been turned into a Bed, Bath, & Beyond store. To go to a movie today in that neighborhood, one can choose from two multiplexes down the road from Summit Mall, containing a total of over 20 screens. About the only thing that is the same as that media experience of 25 years ago is that films are still being projected using emulsion film, but digital film distribution and projection are not far off.

When we went home that night in 1979, very few of us had cable television to watch, and even if we did, the stations available on cable were mostly limited to the three local network affiliates and a couple of local independent stations (which played mostly reruns of old network programming and live broadcasts of Cleveland Indians baseball games). One person in our group did have an amazing device—one of the early Betamax videotape recorders (VCRs)—and we had gone over to his house one evening to watch something he had taped from broadcast television. What a great experience!

To get the soundtrack album for *Manhattan*, we would have had to go to our local record store, where we could buy the album on vinyl or perhaps 8-track cassette, although this latter format was fading away. There was certainly no way to download excerpts to our home computer (which, by the way, none of us had at that point). And, before we went to school on Monday morning in 1979, we might have typed out a paper about the film on a typewriter, but most of us wrote our essays out in longhand. The only way we could have communicated with each other about the film we had just seen was by way of a landline telephone. Very few of us (if any) had our own personal phone lines in our rooms, much less a wireless cell phone, which we would have thought was something out of *Dick Tracy*. There was no way we could have looked up any information about *Manhattan* at home other than what we had available in hard copy either from magazines or newspapers. There certainly was no Internet Movie Database for looking up an actor's name or for communicating with *Manhattan* fans from around the world about the film we had just seen.

The new literacies line of inquiry has been trying to catch up with these staggering changes in media choices that have occurred over the last 25 years and with what they mean for how to define *literacy*. My fascination with a filmmaker's vision would be child's play for the many adolescents who now have their own cell phones and who regularly communicate in chat rooms and via instant messaging with friends and strangers all over the world, while at the same time effortlessly playing games that require them to take on alternate identities. Not only are today's adolescents very cognizant of the fact that a filmmaker is making a statement, they themselves are frequently making multimedia presentations to their classmates at school that often include moving images and sound.

Or are they? I began to wonder how other teachers were using these new literacies in schools, if at all. The intent of this book is to provide portraits of teachers who are struggling to bring new literacies into the traditional K–12 educational system (with the focus of this book being Grades 6 and higher). I searched for teachers who are attempting to do this on a daily basis, with new literacies woven into the regular framework of everything they do. I was not looking for teachers who do a video production unit once a year or who ask their students to do occasional PowerPoint presentations, but rather for teachers who talk with their students every day about all kinds of texts and who together with them become "readers" and "writers" of those various texts. I wondered if there were teachers like this, and if so, how were they doing it? What assignments were they doing? How were they assessing kids in a system that demands that grades be given on some kind of report card? The descriptions of these pioneering classrooms—a result of my 7 years of inquiry—form the essence of this book.

This is an empirical study. The chapters in this book portray teachers and students in their everyday work in school. While this book contains sample assignments and assessments that teachers may choose to implement, it is not designed to be a cookbook for new literacies instruction. My intent, rather, has been to approach this research as a qualitative study, reporting from the field about how teachers are struggling to implement these ideas in the real world of jobs where they may see as many as 100 students a day and must come up with a grade (on a 5-point scale) for each student every 9 weeks. Not only did I want to describe their work, I wanted to hear from teachers and students about their perceptions of this new work.

NEW LITERACY STUDIES AND NEW LITERACIES

Before I could describe these classrooms, I had to find them, and before I could do that, I had to articulate a model or theory of text and text production in order to identify as "a new literacies classroom."

This first chapter provides a record of my starting point as a new literacies scholar, with the intent of making my own perspectives and theoretical points of view explicit as a researcher (Barton & Hamilton, 1998).

As stated, I began to be interested in this line of research because of my own personal interests in nonprint media and my intuition as a teacher that these new literacies were powerful in the classroom. Then I went to the research literature, and next I went out in the field to find other new literacy teachers to describe. This has, therefore, been a recursive process of continually going back and forth from reading and writing about new literacies to seeing instruction with new literacies in the field, all along continually redefining and reconceptualizing my own view of new literacies. Of course, this field of new literacies is actually a rather large umbrella that encompasses many perspectives, and this has added to the challenge of finding these classrooms.

The more I read, the more I saw that there were many different terms being used to talk about the issues surrounding new literacies. It wasn't always clear whether the author's conception of new literacies was the same as mine. Originally, I was interested in film as one of many new literacies available to students today, ranging from instant messaging to 3-D model making. But one of the first authors I read regarding new literacies was David Reinking (1995, 1997) who talked about how even the act of print reading is changing in these new times. Books in the Western tradition, for example, have traditionally been written for the reader to proceed from the front of the book to the back of the book, reading from left to right, and most readers of a book will read the text with the order of the words coming in the same order for him or her as for every other reader of that book. But Reinking talked about how online reading would change the act of reading in that the online reader might click on one hyperlink that another reader would not. The first reader would then proceed through the text in a completely different sequence than the second reader and so on.

While Reinking got me thinking about reading as an increasingly interactive, nonlinear experience, I began to notice that other new literacies writers seemed to be less focused on the gadgets and toys and more on the very notion of literacy as a social process. It seemed that the nature of literacy as an inherently social practice was being talked about as much as were the new technologies. Researchers who focus on new literacies have been going beyond a kind of aesthetic approach or technological determinist approach to new media and symbol systems in which the study is on the auteur. These authors were looking at the "literacy practices" and "literacy events" of the consumers of new literacies. They were interested in mapping these new literacies experiences.

Literacy as a Social Construction

Notions of print reading and writing have been undergoing a reconceptualization as the social nature of language and learning have been emphasized (Vygotsky, 1934/1986; 1978), with *literacy* going from a term that signifies "the ability to read print text" to a more socioculturally mediated practice (Gee, 2000a; Lankshear & Knobel, 2003). "The word is a direct expression of the historical nature of human consciousness," wrote Vygotsky (1934/1986, p. 256). Thus in this world of an increasingly dizzying array of potential reflectors, students need to be able to look at all texts socioculturally (Alvermann & Hagood, 2000; Delpit, 1995; Lankshear, 1997; C. Luke, 2000; Willinsky, 1990).

Gee (2000a) neatly summarized 14 movements that have taken a "massive 'social turn' away from a focus on individual behaviour toward a focus on social and cultural interaction" (p. 180). According to Gee, these 14 movements, in no particular order, are the following: ethnomethodology and conversational analysis; discursive psychology; the ethnography of speaking; sociohistorical psychology; situated cognition; cultural models theory; cognitive linguistics; the new science and technology studies; modern composition theory; connectionism; narrative studies; evolutionary approaches to mind and behavior; modern sociology; and poststructuralism. According to this social perspective, then, literacy is no longer seen as situated only in cognition, to be studied only by psychologists. Literacy is deeply enmeshed in the culture, history, and everyday discourses of people's lives (Barton & Hamilton, 1998; Gee, 1996; Street, 1995). To look at literacy out of these contexts is to miss most (if not all) of what is happening.

This focus on the social practices and events associated with literacy has formed the core of what have become known as the *New Literacy Studies*, which Lankshear and Knobel (2003) define as referring to "a specific sociocultural approach to understanding and researching literacy" (p. 16). It is not that the new technologies are downplayed within New Literacy Studies, although Street (2003) has been critical of what might be termed *multimodal* research for being a throwback to technological determinism, putting too much attention on the medium as determining thought and action. If anything,

the new technologies and their dizzying interactivity and nonlinearity have heightened the need to situate any literacy study firmly within the contexts of the readers and writers being studied, however complex these contexts may be.

As I began to think about searching for teachers who teach new
literacies, Barton and Hamilton's book *Local Literacies* (1998) was
very helpful to me on several levels, both as a model of qualitative
research with its total respect for participants and the setting, and as
a model of looking at "how texts are used: what people did with
them and why and the values these reveal" (p. 216). Furthermore,
building on the work of Brian Street (1995), Barton and Hamilton
wrote about "dominant" and "vernacular" literacies, vernacular literacies being those that give possibilities of participation from more
voices "located in people's networks of support" (p. 253), rather than
a dominant view of literacy that implies a one-size-fits-all approach
to literacy instruction. Street had earlier emphasized that an
"autonomous" model of literacy is problematic, to say the least, and
that a new literacies classroom could be a classroom that celebrates
a vernacular literacy, and, hence, these alternative forms of representation (alternative to print) would necessarily be varied from
classroom to classroom. Researchers in the New Literacy Studies
focus on *literacy practices*, "the general cultural ways of utilizing
written language which people draw upon in their lives. In the sim-
plest sense, literacy practices are what people do with literacy. . .
.Practices are not observable units of behaviour since they also
involve values, attitudes, feelings and social relationships" (Barton
& Hamilton, 1998, p. 6).

If literacy is to be inextricably linked to social context, then linked
to that focus may be criticism of the power structure in that social context, as well as its prevailing discourses (Fairclough, 1989, 1995). As
Rogers (2002) defined this perspective, "Critical literacy concerns itself
with disrupting dominant social practices through resistant reading
and writing of texts" (p. 773). Those who write from a critical literacy
perspective suggest that teachers need to uncover these power dynam-
ics for kids and that all voices in our classrooms need to be allowed to
be heard, regardless of preference of medium (Delpit, 1995; Freire,
1970; McLaren, 1989; Morrell, 2002; Willinsky, 1990).

Mapping Out-of-School and In-School Literacies

If we are going to "unpack levels of texts" and critically examine
discourses, then we are going to have to know what people's literacy
practices are in this wild, new media territory; we will need to map

students' practices and their crossings (transversals) across time, media, and space (Lemke, 2004). Space has become, in fact, a powerful metaphor for critical social theorists in general and specifically as we think about discovering this new frontier of literacies (Soja, 1989, 1996). Lemke (2003) has pointed to the following examples of traversals across space that people routinely make in this new media age: channel surfing, using hypertext links embedded within documents, web surfing, and mall cruising. Gee (2003) has described the hybrid spaces occupied by video game players as they construct alternative identities and write hundreds of words of text in order to inhabit a world marked by immediacy, simultaneity, and nonlinearity. People move increasingly with ease and frequency between online and offline worlds (Beavis & Nixon, 2003; Chandler-Olcott & Mahar, 2003b; Leander, 2003). Studies have attempted to portray students' uses of media and the intertextual lives they lead (Bloome & Egan-Robertson, 1993), "moving the discussion beyond a technocratic view of literacy practices toward an understanding of how digital culture locates adolescents in new ways" (Alvermann, 2002, pp. viii–ix). In sum, we have the beginnings of accumulating ethnographic data that give us portraits, albeit brief and transitory, of the media lives of young people.

But can these out-of-school literacies intersect with students' in-school literacies? After-school learning activities have been shown to allow for learning environments that let a student "author herself or himself into the world as someone empowered" (Blackburn, 2003, p. 314). Because of the lack of pressure to hold to some kind of curriculum standard, after-school programs can move at a different pace, perhaps giving students more space to explore these new terrains intersecting literacies with identity work (Alvermann & Heron, 2001; Hawisher, 2000; Heath, 2001). But what can be done inside of schools to build a bridge to these new literacies?

A few writers have tried to imagine what the new literacies classroom might look like. Some have proposed that new literacies classrooms might be interdisciplinary in nature (Eisner, 1997; Moje, Young, Readence, & Moore, 2000) or more inquiry-based (Bruce, 2002; Bruce & Bishop, 2002; Dewey, 1902/1990) with students becoming apprentices to the teachers who model for their students their own symbol uses (Brown, Collins, & Duguid, 1989). Some have proposed using such new media as rap music and hip-hop culture (Alexander-Smith, 2004; Morrell, 2002; Paul, 2000) or graphic novels and anime (Frey & Fisher, 2004; Morrison, Bryan, & Chilcoat, 2002; Norton, 2003; Versaci, 2001) or pop culture in general (Alvermann,

Moon & Hagood, 1999; Callahan & Low, 2004; Evans, 2004; Maness, 2004) to connect with adolescents who may feel increasingly marginalized by in-school literacies. The phenomenon of *fan fiction*, for example, in which students write and post reams of prose online as fictional characters or compose and post alternative endings to movies or television shows, has been explored as a possible way of linking up in-school goals with out-of-school goals (Chandler-Olcott & Mahar, 2003a).

But should some kind of official curriculum objective be the ulterior motive behind bringing new literacies into the school? Is there a danger that the use of new media in schools will be solely to function as the spoonful of sugar to make the medicine go down? Should the Internet (Leu, 1996, 1997, 2001, 2002; Riel & Fulton, 2001) or email (Blasé, 2000; Doherty & Mayer, 2003; Sipe, 2000; Van Whye, 2000) be brought into the schools mainly to serve the teaching of content, for example, setting up WebQuests (internet scavenger hunts) or email pen pals just to get students talking to each other about Shakespeare? Should new literacy assignments exist for the aim of uncovering racism, sexism, and heterosexism in the popular media (Bean & Moni; 2003; Wallowitz, 2004)? Or are these goals and aims mutually exclusive?

Some of the in-school assignments described to this point could potentially be personally empowering for students, as ways of helping improve print literacies, for example, by using visual art strategies to further print comprehension and general learning (Bustle, 2004; Hibbing & Rankin-Erickson, 2003; Lee, 2003; Short, Harste & Burke, 1996; Short, Kauffman, & Kahn, 2000; Whitin, 2002). In the "sketch-to-stretch" strategy, students are encouraged to translate something they have read in print into a drawing or some other form of visual image. It could be that this kind of visualization could help students comprehend the content more effectively than simply relying on print to convey all of the information (Tsurusaki, Deaton, Hay, & Thomson, 2003). Other studies have compared and contrasted reading and writing strategies for traditional print text versus hypertext (Coiro, 2003; Dreher, 2000; Patterson, 2000; Schmar-Dobler, 2003).

Proponents of the arts in education have always advocated for more media—such as music, theater, and visual arts—in schools. These forms allow for "multiple ways of knowing" (Short & Harste, 1996); the arts (as available symbol systems) can and should be used to teach content and meaning making (Greene, 1997; Leland & Harste, 1994). A popular assignment in the United States has been *multigenre writing*, as developed by Tom Romano (1995, 2000). This format for papers encourages students to approach any topic by composing different pieces such as poetry, song lyrics, or even a want ad or an obituary all related to whatever topic is being explored. Students who write multi-genre papers report coming to know their topics in much richer, more complex ways than they would have, had they written a standard research paper about their topic. Arts education has, in fact, moved away from an emphasis on creative self-expression to what has become known as "discipline-based art education," focusing on not only art making but art history, art criticism, and aesthetics (Greer, 1997; Walling, 2001). In addition to helping students connect with the content, however, arts advocates still feel that encouraging more art forms in our classrooms would allow for a more heightened individual self-realization, so that students can fully explore their own blend of multiple intelligences (Gardner, 1983, 1993, 1995) and fully realize a kind of "cognitive pluralism" (John-Steiner, 1997) that does not limit in any way human thought (Eisner, 1992, 1994, 1997, 2002).

Others have suggested that students need expertise in visual literacy (Gombrich, 1960; Messaris, 1994) to help them cope with the abundant images that deluge life today. Going beyond knowledge of still images, students also need to understand the grammar of motion pictures, and there have been many sources to help educators with this task (Bogdanovich, 1997; Costanzo, 1992; Foster, 2002; Giannetti, 2001; Kerr, 1975; Metz, 1974; Monaco, 2000; Morrell, 2002; Shafer, 2000; Vetrie, 2004; Williams, 2003). Voices from Europe and Australia have been the loudest ones calling ultimately for teaching young people to be "media literate" (Buckingham, 1993, 2003; Buckingham & Sefton-Green, 1994; Lusted, 1991). Both Buckingham (2003) and Hobbs and Frost (2003) have conceptualized media education as including elements of both media production and media consumerism, arguing that students should not only have the ability to cut together a scene without making continuity mistakes, but also to critically view a film as a text, noticing everything from the director's use of lighting and composition to the placement of a Dr. Pepper can sitting just inside the frame. As chronicled by Tyner (1998), information literacy also developed in the 1970s with librarians feeling that students need to be able to sort through all of the bunches of information that are out there. As Tyner points out, "The similarities between the stated competencies of information literacy, visual literacy, and media literacy are so close that separating them seems unnecessarily artificial" (p. 104).

Over the last 10 to 15 years, several models of new literacies pedagogy have been developed. Probably the most famous of these is the pedagogy of Multiliteracies, which breaks the meaning-making process into six design elements and four components of pedagogy (Cope & Kalantzis, 2000; New London Group, 1996). The New London Group (a group of new media scholars originally meeting in New London, Connecticut) proposed teaching children to be able to use what they called the "Available Designs" in a meaningful and critical manner. These "Available Designs . . . include the 'grammars' of various semiotic systems: the grammars of languages, and the grammars of other semiotic systems such as film, photography or gesture. Available Designs also include 'orders of discourse,' . . . the structured set of conventions associated with semiotic activity . . . in a given social space" (New London Group, 1996, p. 74). The pedagogy of Multiliteracies suggests that students need to know all of the Available Designs that can be used to "write" in all contexts and that depriving students of the designs that should be available to them deprives them of a seat at the table of literacies in this increasingly multimodal society. Other models of multiliteracy teaching, such as Green's Three Dimensions model (1988) and the Four Resources model of Freebody and Luke (1990), have conceptualized literacy in these new times as consisting of both functional-operational levels and critical analysis levels (Nixon, 2003). In sum, students should be able to both read critically and write functionally, no matter what the medium.

But, in the end, what is the sixth-grade teacher who is interested in new literacies to do on a Monday morning? How is a teacher supposed to do all of this—especially if the teacher desires to teach new literacies in a systemic, everyday way? I found excellent online sources, such as the George Lucas Foundation's Edutopia (www.glef.org), the Media Awareness Network (www.media-awareness.ca), and the Center for Media Literacy (www.medialit.org), that provided more ideas for specific new literacies assignments. But I still wondered if there were teachers who were attempting to go beyond one-shot assignments and weave new literacies into the fabric of their classrooms. And if I were to attempt to find such classrooms, how would I know when I had found what I was looking for? To begin with, I didn't even know what to call the kind of teaching I was attempting to describe.

TERMINOLOGY

In writing about this area of research, one is challenged when deciding what to call it: "new literacies," "new literacy," "multiliteracies," "media literacy," "critical multimedia literacy," or even "aesthetic literacy." As discussed, the word *new* has been attached to the word *literacy* both for paradigmatic reasons (the shift to socio-cultural approaches to literacy) and for ontological and chronological reasons (Lankshear & Knobel, 2003).

But the use of the word *literacy* has also been controversial. At the recent Ghent conference on multiliteracies (*Multiliteracies: The Contact Zone*, September 22–27, 2003, sponsored by the Scientific Commission on Literacy of the Association Internationale de Linguistique Appliquee), some participants expressed perplexity that the term *literacy* has been attached to other words to form terms such as *computer literacy, emotional literacy,* and even *sexual literacy*. Some scholars feel that *literacy* is a term that should be attached only to reading and writing. (But one could ask, "Reading and writing of what kinds of texts? Should working in print text be the only reading and writing that is privileged to be called *literacy?*") Others at the Ghent conference pointed out that in most other languages, there are no words similar to *literacy* that can be attached to other concepts (such as computer or emotional) to make a new phrase.

I have decided to follow the lead of the New Literacy Studies in that, when I am referring to the approach and perspective that situates literacy clearly as a social practice, I will use and capitalize New Literacy. When I am referring to the plethora of communication media available today, I will call these new literacies and not capitalize. There will occasionally be times in the text when I use (or one of the people I'm quoting uses) the term *multiliteracies*. This should not signify that I am referring to any different concept than what I will in most cases refer to as new literacies. I (and the teachers profiled in this book) are essentially ascribing to a broadened definition of literacy, similar to Eisner's:

> In order to be read, a poem, an equation, a painting, a dance, a novel, or a contract each requires a distinctive form of literacy, when literacy means, as I intend it to mean, a way of conveying meaning through and recovering meaning from the form of representation in which it appears. (1997, p. 353)

My only quibble with the Eisner definition is that I would substitute the word *constructing* for *recovering* in that I believe a reader constructs meaning based on his or her own life experiences in transaction with a text. Also, it is worth noting that I am holding to a concept of new literacies that is not wholly dependent on technology—that is, as Eisner states, even such "old fashioned" forms as dance and painting can be "read" and "written." In short, there should be no form of representation that is not embraced or is out of favor in this world that is becoming dominated by textually mediated worlds such as games and chat rooms that are more transitory in nature. For this reason, I also like Alvermann's (2002) definition of a broadened notion of literacies "to include the performative, visual, aural, and semiotic understandings necessary for constructing and reconstructing print- and nonprint-based texts" (p. viii). Finally, in most cases, I will not put quotation marks around the words reading and writing and will always intend these words to mean *reading* and *writing* using any form of representation.

I came to this line of research because of my interest in these new literacies. I soon found that I was becoming immersed in a New Literacy perspective—a larger approach to literacy in general that is completely contextualized in social practices—and that this approach has immense implications for teachers, policymakers, and researchers. Lankshear and Knobel (2003) argue that "it is time that literacy scholars working from a New Literacy Studies perspective begin to engage much more seriously with new literacies" (p. 18). And, indeed, even though I had begun my study of new literacies classrooms before I had read this statement, I believe that my study is an attempt at forging that tie between theory and practice.

RESEARCHING NEW LITERACIES CLASSROOMS

Although my *Manhattan* experience was out of school, this is a book set squarely in schools. They are not conventional classrooms, but they are in conventional middle schools and high schools. The teachers and students profiled herein are working to survive and thrive in a world that increasingly puts emphasis on one's ability to work in multiple forms of representation across a wide variety of spaces, all text-driven in one way or another. The challenge faced by these teachers is that they are working within an organizational system that couldn't care less about crossing boundaries. In fact, the emphasis is on staying inside the lines.

Goal of the Study

My goal has been to share the work of classroom teachers and students (with their permission) who attempt to weave new literacies into everyday life in their classrooms. These teachers do more than one new literacies assignment per year or per semester. For these teachers, using new literacies is not a one-time stunt, or something to be done as a reward, or something to calm down at-risk students. I have set out to find and describe the work of these teachers, not in a recipe fashion, but almost as an anthropological study, taking oral histories, as Kevin Brownlow (1968) did with aging silent film actors and directors. I have collected artifacts and stories from new literacies classrooms at the beginning of the twenty-first century. For these pioneering teachers and students, new literacies has become a part of everyday classroom life.

My study will help to fill the gap noted by Nixon (2003), who wrote that "there have been very few studies of critical and transformative new media literacy practices within school-based education" (p. 409). The chapters in this book chronicle the work of teachers who are attempting—sometimes against a rising tide of indifference and even hostility—to change "the relationships between the school, the home, and the community" (Leander, 2003, p. 393). How can teachers transform their classrooms into ones where these boundaries are crossed regularly and where "people make meaning across multiple media, multiple attentional foci, multiple sites, and multiple timescales?" (Lemke, 2004). Indeed, Lemke suggests that rather than asking the question, How do people learn?, we should be asking the question, How do we learn more about how people use space and place, time and pace in activity and learning?

Some of the teachers in this book (at Parma High) have put an emphasis on the study of symbol systems and how they can be used across media in both abstract and literal fashion. One teacher has used new technology to allow students to cross over to the community to chronicle the people of the community, making a homegrown Hollywood (ironically in the backyard of Hollywood itself). Another teacher outside of Montreal has used new technologies to cross the borders of literacy in an at-risk, bilingual setting. Another group of teachers (an English department at a high school in Calgary) has used multiple forms of representation to allow students to express themselves creatively in a standards-based, test-driven environment. In a rural self-contained eighth-grade classroom, a teacher has used new literacies to cross the barriers of extreme isolation. Finally, a middle school librarian has used new literacies to break down the borders of content area discipline territories. Interestingly, one of the findings of this book is that these pioneering teachers put a great deal of emphasis on teaching the process of working, inevitably including a great deal of collaborative work, above the product.

Make no mistake, the teachers profiled in this book have struggled; some of the classrooms profiled in this book no longer exist as of this writing. These are teachers who have chosen to blaze a new literacies trail for us, and it has not always been easy or according to plan. These teachers and students are trying to do something very different.

Before I went off to find these classrooms, I had to acknowledge that life as a literacy researcher had changed (Hagood, 2003). Many of the classrooms I researched, I first met online, and our first dialogues were via email. Some of the first classroom work I saw from these teachers was via attachments sent to me electronically, although I knew that I would eventually have to represent the work of these teachers and students mostly using words and numbers: a dilemma facing today's educational research (Fischman, 2001).

Based on a review of the literature that has appeared elsewhere (Kist, 2000), I developed five defining characteristics of a new literacies classroom. These characteristics (see Figure 1.1) served as a starting point for finding classrooms that feature a broadened definition of literacy.

The challenge for this project was how to determine whether a classroom was really a new literacies classroom. To be chosen for case study research, I felt the classroom needed to show evidence, during follow-up phone interviews and observations, of exhibiting at least three of the five characteristics of new literacies classrooms. Over a 2-year period, I gathered nominations for almost 60 new literacies classrooms, with the help of scholars in the field, many electronic mailing lists, and colleagues in many locales.

Throughout this time of gathering nominations, I continued to do follow-up phone interviews. I was enjoying the conversations, but I was having increasing doubts about my survey instrument (see Appendix, "New Literacy Classroom Characteristic Scale"). So, about a third of the way through the phone interviewing, I abandoned the formal survey but kept the general intent of the questions, usually starting the conversation by simply asking teachers to describe some of their assignments. Sometimes a teacher would be disqualified by saying something like, "You should come to visit in 6 weeks when I do my Van Gogh sunflower unit." The first characteristic on my list was that these classrooms should feature daily work in multiple forms of representation. When teachers described one-time units, I knew that alternative media were not featured on a regular basis in their classrooms. Throughout the phone interviews, I also felt that a key tip-off was whether the teacher mentioned talking about symbol systems or texts with students. When this was the case, I felt that I was closer to finding a true new literacies classroom, because here was a teacher who realized that explicit discussion of symbol systems was itself a worthy curriculum goal. On the other

FIGURE 1.1 Characteristics of New Literacies Classrooms

- Classrooms feature daily work in multiple forms of representation.
- There are explicit discussions of the merits of using certain symbol systems in certain situations with much choice (Eisner, 1994, 1997; Greeno & Hall, 1997; New London Group, 1996).
- There are metadialogues by the teacher who models working through problems using certain symbol systems (Tishman & Perkins, 1997).
- Students take part in a mix of individual and collaborative activities (John-Steiner, 1997).
- Classrooms are places of student engagement in which students report achieving a "flow" state (Csikszentmihalyi, 1990, 1991, 1993).

hand, I was sometimes dismayed by teachers who would proclaim that they were new literacies teachers because they assigned PowerPoint oral presentations for their students to do. The mere presence of technology in a classroom was not one of my criteria for categorizing a classroom as a new literacies classroom. Further, the ability to spout a professional research base was not a guarantee of inclusion. In one case, I made an out-of-state visit to a very well known school and almost immediately determined that their extensive research base had not led to a true manifestation of the five characteristics of new literacies that I was using. (One clue was that one of the teachers kept yelling at a student to "Quit singing!") They may have talked the talk on the phone, but they were not walking the walk in person.

The Cases

This almost 7-year long process has resulted in the following 6th- to 12th-grade profiles for this book:

- An 11th- to 12th-grade interdisciplinary, Western civilization class outside of Cleveland, Ohio, cotaught by a language arts teacher, a music teacher, and an art teacher
- A self-contained 8th-grade classroom in rural Manitoba, Canada, where students use multiliteracies to conduct real-world interdisciplinary projects
- A high school social studies/computer teacher and an English teacher in San Fernando City, part of the Los Angeles school system, who have used digital media to inspire students' pride in themselves and in the community

- A media specialist in an affluent middle school outside of Chicago who helps her teams of teachers infuse multiliteracies throughout the school and maintain an interdisciplinary focus
- An alternative high school outside of Montreal, Quebec, Canada, that uses a new literacies curriculum to reach out to at-risk 9th and 10th graders who come from a variety of backgrounds, both English- and French-speaking
- A high school English Department in Calgary, Alberta, Canada, that has students reading various media texts revolving around a theme and responding to those texts in a great variety of media, embedding student choice of form of representation into every assignment

When conceptualizing this study, I did not intend to find a variety of examples, such as urban, rural, and suburban new literacies classrooms, or one that featured a school librarian. I did want to find classrooms beyond my home state of Ohio, but beyond that, my main intent was to find what I believed to be true new literacies classrooms. I also found eligible elementary classrooms but chose to concentrate in this book upon the secondary level of schooling.

Most of the teachers profiled in this book have never been written about before and have never been published themselves. They are not interested in becoming superstars of new literacies, and very few have read the work of the New London Group (1996) or Brian Street (1995) or any of the other New Literacy scholars. Nor have they necessarily been influenced by professional organizations' legitimization of new literacies (Commission on Adolescent Literacy, 1999; NCTE/IRA, 1996). The teachers described in these chapters are just doing it, for reasons that even they find sometimes difficult to articulate, with the result that they frequently feel isolated and set apart from the mainstream of their own school cultures. These are simply teachers of middle school and high school who have decided, for multiple reasons, to broaden the conception of literacy in their classrooms. This book describes how they took these pioneering steps.

The Research

My research questions for the study have been:

1. How do teachers teach who teach in new literacies classrooms?
   a. What are the assignments that new literacies teachers are making?

   b. What do assessments look like in new literacies classrooms?
2. What are students' and teachers' perceptions of their experiences in these different classrooms?

I set up an observation schedule that allowed me to be present in each classroom for 2 to 5 consecutive days (except for the Chicago school where, due to unforeseen circumstances, I was able to spend only one day). My data collecting consisted of scripting and taking rough field notes as well as videotaping during the observations with more elaboration filled in as soon as possible after the observation (Merriam, 1998). In most of the classrooms, I also shot videotape of selected events.

Extensive interviews were conducted with the teachers, first via phone and email before my visit, next in person in the evening or weekend during my school observations, and then often via phone or email after my return home. All interviews were taped. For each teacher, I would often begin by asking some background questions such as, What led you to teach in this manner? I would also ask completely open-ended questions such as, What have you noticed in your classroom as a result? The conversation that ensued often led us to discuss some of the issues raised by the research questions.

In the student interviews, I also began with somewhat of an open-ended question such as, What do you notice that's different about this class from other classes? What do you think about that difference? I then asked questions such as, How does this type of instruction help you make meaning? What do you notice about the way you work in this classroom? What do you notice about the way you learn in this classroom? How is it different from the way you learn in other classrooms? I would also ask students to characterize their "best" learning experience, even if it was not in the classroom I was studying, and to talk about a time when they were completely engrossed in their work. I also asked both students and teachers about the assignments that were given in the classroom.

On average, over 60 pages of single-spaced pages of data were accumulated for each site plus hours of digital video and many online artifacts. As I analyzed the data, I found myself emulating the collaborative ethnography described by Barton and Hamilton (1998), as I have emailed or phoned many of the teacher participants throughout the writing of this book. All participants have also read relevant chapters at least once during the writing process, and some twice, in order to provide member checking and an assurance that I have portrayed their classrooms fairly. Inductive analysis took place throughout and after the data collection process to identify data congruent with the research goals and to uncover categories and refine categories via the constant comparative method (Glaser & Strauss, 1967). For a more complete description of my data analysis methods, see Kist (2002).

In the end, no study is perfect. As Barton and Hamilton have said, "It is important to stress that other people's voices have always been mediated by us" (1998, p. 72). Like them, I have made every attempt to fairly select and describe these classrooms. Any praise should go to the teachers and their work, while any criticism should come to me.

The following six chapters each contain a description of the classroom studied as well as some sample assignments and assessments. I have decided to use the real names of the teachers and schools I am profiling, similar to Wood (1992), because I would like for them to receive credit for all the work they have done. However, I have changed the names of the students quoted. In the closing chapter, I provide an overview of trends of the data as well as my perspective at the end of this journey, even as new questions are generated.

WHAT'S NEW IN NEW LITERACIES?

It is ironic that, as I prepare the final draft of this book on new literacies, I am visiting a very old city in Europe: Ghent (Gent), Belgium. Ghent was founded in the seventh century between the rivers Scheide and Leie in the Flanders section of Belgium. At that time Ghent was part of the kingdom of Burgundy and, after several hundred years, the town hit its peak in the thirteenth and fourteenth centuries when it became a leader in textile production. Now, in the midst of this medieval setting, over 100 New Literacy scholars are discussing multiliteracies at a meeting of the Association Internationale de Linguistique Appliquée (AILA). And here I sit with my laptop looking over at the Cathedral of St. Bavo (St. Baaf), construction of which began in 1300.

Gunther Kress is one of the keynote speakers at this conference. In his latest book, *Literacy in the New Media Age* (2003), Kress writes,

It is no longer possible to think about literacy in isolation from a vast array of social, technological and economic factors. Two distinct yet related factors deserve to be particularly highlighted. These are, on the one hand, the broad move from the now centuries-long dominance of writing to the new dominance of the image and, on the other hand, the

move from the dominance of the medium of the book to the dominance
of the medium of the screen. (p. 1)

But is the dominance of the image really that new? Between conference sessions, I have managed to get in some tourist time, and one
of the first places I visited was the Cathedral of St. Bavo, located on
the town square, which contains many works of art from the
Romanesque, high Gothic, and late Gothic periods. A painting by
Rubens (*The Conversion of St. Bavo*), dating from 1623, is owned by
the church. I was looking at this painting when a docent walked over
with a group to talk about this painting and the different elements of
visual symbolism that were contained in it, including Rubens's well-
known diagonal sweep of composition.

To make a long story short, soon I was following this docent all
over the cathedral and the lower crypt as I listened to her fascinating
explanation of the complex visual communication inherent in these
artworks, including a two-story carved rococo pulpit with characters
representing "Truth triumphing over evil"; a complex triptych
depicting the crucifixion of Christ; and the cathedral's famous painting, *The Adoration of the Lamb*, a masterpiece of the Flemish primitive school, painted by the Van Eyck brothers, Jan and Hubert.
Finished in 1432, each of the panels of this polytych is spectacularly
painted and contains various characters from the Bible as well as certain symbols from the Bible, Greek mythology, and even pagan characters (who people of the time felt had predicted the advent of
Christianity). Some citizens of the town of that time also appear in
the panels (Schmidt, 2001).

The docent also explained the "obit" system in which a well-
known person is buried in the crypt under a sign with a complex
symbolic coat of arms represented, a sign system that was so clearly
understood by the people of its time that no name of the deceased
was necessary on the obit. Everyone knew who was buried there by
looking at the symbols on the obit. When I asked her how she learned
all this "stuff," she paused and said, "How does one learn to
breathe?" She went on to say, "This is my city. . . . We are proud of
these things."

After my tour, as I sat on the town square, eating my waterzooi,
I thought about the level of symbol using that I had seen demonstrated by these artists from hundreds of years ago. I thought about
the townspeople of the fifteenth century who donated the money for
the artwork and the townspeople who still volunteer to conduct
impromptu tours of the buildings of which they are justifiably proud.

I thought of how the townspeople of the town understood the symbols that the Van Eyck brothers had painted without having to buy a book or listen to a taped commentary. I thought of the pride of ownership the docent demonstrated in these works of art and her deep level of symbolic understanding—"How does one learn to breathe?"

Sitting in Ghent, I felt surrounded by a time period before the screen: when the dominant medium was also visual, but the images were painted on canvas or woven into tapestries or worked into sculpture. The conference proceedings had my head swimming with the implications for how the new textual worlds of identity-driven games and holographic imagery, for example, will transform everyday classrooms. But, looking around this old city, I wondered if we have really come to terms with fully engaging with the old textual worlds of triptychs and statues. It seems that the people of this medieval city were swimming in imagery as much as we are swimming in emoticons. I am certainly not the first person to think about the non-newness of alternative symbol systems (Bruce, 2002; Resnick, 1991), but being in such an old European city served as a reminder of our long human history that has been enmeshed with all kinds of print and nonprint symbol making.

In the classrooms I have studied, a shift in emphasis to "text" and "symbol system" has already begun, and I hope that this book will add to a dialogue surrounding what these new literacies may look like in practice. Yet again, ironically, being in such an old city as I finish writing this study has caused me to problematize the notion of a "broadened conception of literacy," and I find myself thinking back to the docent who is quite conversant in the old language of image-based communication. Has there ever been a time when we have not been awash in a remarkable torrent of symbols and opportunities for reading and writing them?

Chapter 2

TRANSLATION AND FLUENCY IN AN URBAN HIGH SCHOOL INTERDISCIPLINARY CLASSROOM

Profile: William Peck, Richard Zasa, and James Sentz
Parma High School, Parma, Ohio

During the 1960s, local Cleveland TV horror movie host "Ghoulardi" would mercilessly make fun of the Cleveland suburb of Parma. In fact, white socks to this day are still referred to as "Parmas" in northeast Ohio, because Ghoulardi always pointed out the apparent fact that people from Parma wear white socks regardless of the shoes they are wearing. Ghoulardi forever stamped Parma as being the ultimate of uncool, filled not only with white socks, but also with people who love to go bowling, eat polish sausage (kielbasa), and put pink plastic flamingos in their front yards. Famous Clevelander Drew Carey has used "Moon Over Parma" as one of his television show's theme songs: "Moon over Parma, bring my love to me tonight. Guide her to Cleveland, underneath your silvery light. We're going bowlin', so don't lose her in Solon. Moon over Parma, tonight!" (McGuire, 1995).

I thought of this as I drove through the blue-collar neighborhoods

Portions of this chapter originally appeared in "Finding 'New Literacy' in Action: An Interdisciplinary High School Western Civilization Class," by W. Kist, 2002, *Journal of Adolescent & Adult Literacy, 45,* pp. 368–377.

of Parma in the late 1990s to see a new literacies classroom at Parma High School. I would find that this uncoolest of suburbs contained some of the coolest new literacies assignments and assessments I'd seen. Interestingly, however, this classroom was not dominated by technology or new media. In fact, except for using the Internet for research purposes, students spent most of their creative efforts making art and music projects. What perhaps most marked this classroom as a new literacies classroom was that teachers and students were using these nonprint media to break out of lecture-based, paper-and-pencil assessed methods traditionally used to cover this kind of college prep content. It was very clear to the students I interviewed that this class was unlike any other that they had at Parma High School.

A NONTRADITIONAL CLASS

A group of seven male high school students sits around a table in a dusty classroom of this urban high school. Gary is talking animatedly about their project with the other students. "The setting is almost supernatural. I want to create that," he says. The other students are quiet. Hal speaks up: "I think what we had was a decent idea." A quiet student named Bruce says, "We were going to use those balls—the biggest one goes on top. His own world is way over there." Bruce gestures out into space, high into the air. "So it makes sense, but at the same time . . . we need a base. . . . It's not going to hold it up." Tom says, "Color is another thing we have to decide." Now all the students talk on top of each other:
"Having it on the top shows the importance . . ."
"We're allowed to fold shapes, too."
"The top one should be neon, hot pink."
"Why is 'love' above 'friendliness'?"
"We can't assume what his emotions were."
"[We can] . . . from his books."
"The top one could be his love for education."
"It would make a lot of sense then."
"We should label each ball."

This last comment leads to a spirited discussion of whether each ball should be explicitly labeled, or if that goes against the spirit of the assignment.

The name of the class these students were taking was Arts Seminar, and the students were working to design a monument to a person, event, or a phenomenon. This group of students had selected to pay tribute to Dr. Seuss. The challenge of the assignment was that the monument could not be figurative in nature—the students could not, for example, erect a sculpture of Dr. Seuss's physical likeness, or of one of the characters from his books. The monument had to be designed in a completely abstract fashion, using shapes such as spheres, hence the discussion in which students were debating what each of the balls could represent of the life of Dr. Seuss.

As discussed in the first chapter, there continue to be many different perspectives on new literacies curricula. The teachers profiled in this chapter have redesigned their course to be interdisciplinary in nature (Eisner, 1997; Moje, Young, Readence, & Moore, 2000) with an emphasis on the role of the arts in teaching both academic content and meaning making in general (Greene, 1997; Leland & Harste, 1994). Yet the three teachers profiled here constructed their new literacies classroom without ever having been exposed to any research or writings about new literacies. They completely refashioned a lecture-based course, partly due to administrative fiat, but also because of their own restlessness and sense that the course could be better. I visited this classroom at regular intervals during parts of 2 school years (1997–98 and 1998–99). This chapter presents the story of the three teachers who cotaught Arts Seminar and who developed all of the assignments and rubrics for the course themselves.

THE SETTING

Parma High School is situated in a large, sprawling building in the middle of Parma, a working-class suburb of Cleveland. The school is set in a neighborhood of well-kept homes that sometimes look as if they have seen better days. I've never seen a pink flamingo in a front yard. The neighborhood and the school have become increasingly diverse over the years, no longer dominated by Polish and other Middle European Americans.

Arts Seminar is a class that has been offered in Parma schools for at least 30 years, according to Bill Peck, one of the class's teachers. In the late 1990s, the course was being team-taught by Peck, an art teacher; Jim Sentz, a music teacher; and Rich Zasa, an English teacher. The class was usually offered one period a day with over 50 students in the class. During the 1998–99 school year, when I observed the class, there were 75 students in the class.

Arts Seminar had traditionally been an elective, arts credit course for college-prep juniors and seniors. Its purpose has been to give an overview of Western civilization from the perspective of great writers, artists, and musicians. For many years, the art teacher, music teacher, and English teacher took turns lecturing to the whole group for one or more days while the other two teachers would take a less prominent role, sometimes interrupting with clarifying (or even sarcastic) commentary.

In the mid-1990s, the teachers of Arts Seminar received a mandate from administrators in the school district that the course should be taught differently. The administrators were upset that there was too much downtime with two of the three teachers not doing much while the other teacher lectured. As Zasa explains it, this coincided with the arrival of a new principal in their building who wanted to make some changes and who provided some staff development opportunities. About this time Parma became a member of the Coalition of Essential Schools (http://www.essentialschools.org) and teachers were provided with several one-day workshops conducted by Marian Leibowitz and Theodore Sizer on authentic assessment and curriculum mapping. These in-service courses got the teachers thinking about trying more of a project-based Arts Seminar.

Another impetus for change was that Zasa had cotaught a "block class," which was essentially a double period of language arts with another language arts teacher. With longer periods, "we were also realizing that we couldn't teach the block the same way we had taught previously," explained Zasa. Sentz recalled their decision to change:

> We met in August, talked about the situation . . . basically what they had wanted was the three of us to just split up the class. . . . And we decided with the information [our principal] had sent to us, we were just going to change the whole thing, do curriculum mapping and decide what units we wanted to focus on, what type of project-based or authentic assessment we were going to use. We decided to jump right in and do it.

A key component for making it work was that the principal arranged for Zasa, Peck, and Sentz to have a common planning period, which the teachers said was necessary to do the amount of planning they would have to do to revamp the course. "And it helped that we knew each other," Zasa said. "I think this would be very difficult for three teachers who hadn't worked together before."

"Or even just one person," Peck added. "One person to do it alone is a very difficult job, because you can easily become discouraged if it doesn't work." And, as Peck has recently recalled, going from taking turns lecturing to this new format was not always easy. He remembered some of the first questions they asked themselves:

> How do you change the course from lecture to something else? What will the "else" look like? Is chronology important? What content areas will be discussed? Who gets to do what? We are all strong personalities and there was some territorial spraying that went on. Figurative chairs were thrown and "harrumphs" were muttered. It was not always pretty, and I'm not proud of what I said sometimes. Our mutual respect served us well in the long run, and our course was stronger by the process. . . . I think. It's not easy inventing the wheel.

Gradually, however, the new Arts Seminar curriculum began to evolve. By the 1997–98 school year when I first observed the class, the teachers were into their third year of teaching the revamped Arts Seminar. Although the three teachers had no knowledge of the new literacies movement, I felt they clearly were designing their classrooms to be representationally diverse, reflective, and sometimes explicitly critical.

ELEMENTS OF ARTS SEMINAR

The newly remodeled class became organized around collaborative projects. All projects began with questions such as, "What is a masterpiece?" "Why do we create?" or "What constitutes greatness in the arts?" There were also such questions as, "What is Love?" and "What is Beauty?" Zasa, Peck, and Sentz developed these projects and questions themselves. Students were graded on both individual and collaborative elements of each project. What follows is a discussion of each of the elements of the new Arts Seminar.

Project-Based Classroom Work

The class work was entirely based on collaborative projects, each of which began with a question, and these questions were, by design, higher level questions. Zasa said, "With a low-level question, you already know the answer, so why look? (Instead), we start with a question such as, 'Why do humans create?'" Zasa explained that they generated the questions by "starting with the end in mind—What we start with (is)—what do we want them to learn? What do we hope they will learn? And that discussion . . . generates for us the standards that we use to evaluate the product." For instance, to answer a question such as, "What is Love?" the students would be expected to do readings of different texts in different media related to love and then make a product to present to the audience. Starting with the end in mind was not something the three were used to doing in the earlier days of Arts Seminar. Zasa also noted that in the past they had never surveyed prior knowledge at the start of a unit. Now this became something they did on a regular basis.

I first observed Arts Seminar during the 1997–98 school year, which was the third year of this new version of the course. During most of the time I observed that year, students were working in groups on the Virtual Museum project. The assignment was to create a scheme for an art exhibition: a 3-D model of the exhibit space along with a presentation to the class and accompanying research materials. The original assignment sheet that was given to students appears in Figure 2.1.

The students were first taken to a "real" museum and given questions to answer that would prepare them for creating their own "virtual" museums. The questions asked the students to look at the entire art exhibit as a communication medium itself (as its own form of representation) and to consider its overall impact on the visitor. Some examples of questions were, "What do you notice about the lighting, colors, furnishings, space?" and "How is the viewer conducted through the exhibit?"

During these first observations, I did not see a single lecture. Students were usually working on their projects. Also, I rarely observed them in the same classroom twice. Sometimes they were in the art room, working on their museum models. Sometimes they were in the library doing research. Once, I observed in the band room, when the class was listening to music from various periods in history. Finally, I observed in a standard English classroom as they worked to prepare their presentations.

Student-Led Research

Once students were given the project assignment, the first step was going to the library to do some preliminary research on the topic. In fact, doing research was a primary focus of the new Arts Seminar.

FIGURE 2.1 Virtual Museum Project Assignment Sheet

Essential Question: What considerations are made in the creation and/or setup of an art museum exhibition?

Each group will create a scheme for an art exhibition

1. A 3-D model of the exhibit space that indicates how the elements are displayed.
2. Large examples of individual works that are selected for the exhibit.
3. A written tour that provides factual information for visitors.
4. An oral report to the class highlighting some of your considerations—purpose of the exhibit; works examined; why they were chosen or eliminated; reasons for the setup.
5. Visitor movement and participation and justification.

An account of the research must be submitted individually in a folder

1. Time management log—a record of how you used your time.
2. Research notes with an accounting of *your* research and *your* contributions.
3. A list of the works you selected, rejected, and *why*. Each person will need to research at least six works. Ultimately, each member will choose two that will be included in the finished presentation.
4. A process report.
5. Individual note cards of your part in the presentation.

The presentation

1. Everyone must participate equally.
2. All participants need to know each other's material.
3. If you are absent on the day you are to present, you will do the *entire* presentation for us during an activity period.

Types of exhibits

1. Private collection.
2. Single artist.
3. Regional style.
4. Stylistic period—baroque, impressionism, and so forth.
5. Unique phenomenon—Holocaust art, monastery that produced great stuff, treasure discovered in a cave, Marilyn, and Elvis.

Students were encouraged not only to do research but to evaluate sources seriously and to reflect on their own research processes. As seen in Figure 2.2, the midterm for the class contained questions that asked students to reflect on the research process as well as to relate what they had specifically learned from their own research and that of classmates.

For the three teachers, a crucial part of the research element of the class was helping students learn to evaluate all kinds of different sources. In this aspect, Arts Seminar taught some information literacy skills such as selecting and evaluating research sources (Tyner, 1998). For almost all assignments, students were expected to turn in a group research folder, with evidence of research and a description of how research sources were chosen (see Figure 2.3).

Zasa, Peck, and Sentz began to notice an improvement in their students' abilities to evaluate sources of information since the transformation of Arts Seminar. Zasa felt that in the old Arts Seminar students didn't make judgments about validity of information, they just copied down anything that had to do with the topic that was being researched, "just looking at an encyclopedia and just spouting that information back." Sentz added, "Nowadays, in our electronic age where there are so many sources of information, . . . they're coming out of our class . . . a little more prepared." Zasa also said that they attempted to get students to draw conclusions from the material they find, that the teachers wanted to see "evidence of actual thought." The three teachers felt that the new Arts Seminar made a difference in their students' abilities to cope with the rising tide of information.

Although the teachers designed the questions in the class, students had some ownership over how their research and inquiry were going to proceed. "I think I learn a lot more because of the groups and the projects we do," student Colin stated. "I think it's because you're putting all the information in your own hands and you're doing something with it." The combination of research and application was important to the students according to interview transcripts. Colin felt they learned about abstraction from actually making an abstract object after researching various artists: After doing the research, students got to step inside the shoes of the artist and see what it is like to actually communicate in abstract form. There were students, however, who worried that they were not learning as much content in this project-driven course. A student named Hal was concerned that the project base of the course meant that students only learn the content of the information surrounding the project on which they're working.

FIGURE 2.2 Arts Seminar Midterm

We would like you to respond to three questions about your work in this class so far. Your responses must be in essay/paragraph form. You will have the weekend to begin to organize your thoughts regarding the three questions.

Please answer the following questions completely and thoroughly. Use specific examples when responding to these issues. Vague generalizations do not tell the depth of your learning or understanding. A statement such as "I learned that Japanese art is really very interesting and exciting with many different forms of expression" tells us nothing about your learning. A statement such as "I learned that haiku poetry relates directly to the Buddhist tea ceremony and produced significant pottery developments such as raku" puts a finer point on the substance of the learning.

  1. Discuss the research process. What does it mean? How does it work?
  2. What did you learn from the research of other people in this class? Give examples and be specific! (E.g., "Lo Mein painted multicolored screens, which chronicled the accomplishments of the emperors during the Suung Dynasty. His great reputation brought him fame and security until he died at the age of 87 in 1765.")
  3. What did you learn from your own research? We're looking for content here.

Culminating Presentations in Multiple Forms

Work in multiple forms was ongoing in the new Arts Seminar. There was always a culminating activity at the end of every project, and this culminating activity included some kind of presentation that was usually created in part utilizing one or more nonprint media.

Peck, Sentz, and Zasa sometimes structured the projects so that students used media in which they had no (apparent) expertise. "We made it a rule that everybody participates in everything," Peck said. "Everybody draws; everybody sings." Assignments were carefully structured so that everyone could participate. For example, in the Monument Project (described in full below) all students were given the same geometrical shapes to use in constructing an abstract work. Beyond the content reasons for requiring students to work in the abstract, all students were given the same raw material so that the group could not be dominated by the best figurative artist in the group.

In the case of the music project, each group had to perform an original composition as part of their presentation. Sentz described the project as follows:

FIGURE 2.3 Research Folder Assessment Rubric

1. One folder per group
2. Evidence of research (written record of choices)
3. Source information (where did you look?)
4. Evidence: How did you apply criteria?
5. Show how you selected your three choices
6. Abstract of presentation content
7. Collaborative learning evaluations

4 (Above and Beyond) 50 points

1. Written record of research: each work considered in detail, 5 each or more
2. Works cited information (used more than 4 resources)
3. Chart showing how indicators were applied to each considered work
4. Evidence of evaluation process
5. Final choices and why
6. Group performance evaluation
7. Abstract of presentation

3 (What Is Expected) 44–40 points

1. Written record of research: each work considered in detail, 5 each
2. Works cited (at least 3 sources)
3. Evidence of how indicators are applied
4. How final 3 were selected
5. Group performance evaluation
6. Outline of presentation

2 (Average) 40-20 points

1. List of works included, but lacks details; process of selection not clear
2. Works cited (fewer than 3 used)
3. Final choices indicated but lacks process information
4. Group evaluations included
5. Outline of presentation needs detail

1 (Below Average) 20-0 points

1. Missing a required element
2. Choices not considered fully
3. Final choice indicators not explained
4. Group evaluations present but not completed
5. Final presentation outline needs completion

Each particular group had at least one person who had some kind of musical background. So I came up with 16 different orchestral excerpts. [Two members of the group] had to provide some sort of rhythmic accompaniment for that particular excerpt. . . . The other two students who were left had to do research . . . . This developed into a presentation where students would play the excerpt, other students would get up and talk about the piece, and then they would play the original composition.

Zasa recalled, "I just thought this was a remarkable experience for all of them—to have to get up. We're in a choir room and do this in front of everyone. Especially those kids who hadn't any performance experience." Sentz mentioned the presentation aspect of the projects as being of special benefit to some of their at-risk students who were "developing more confidence, and some of that comes from just a presentation mode of standing up in front of their peers and having to have enough information and background that they can communicate that."

Assessment of Product and Process

Students in Arts Seminar were graded on each component of the project, including the presentation itself, group research folder, individual time management logs, and a process report in which they are supposed to describe the entire process that was gone through in preparation of the final assignment. The three teachers used rubrics to evaluate each section of each project. Each teacher evaluated each project, and then the three teachers reached agreement on what the final grade would be.

In addition to the projects, at the end of the semester, instead of a traditional multiple-choice assessment, students were asked to reflect back over what they had learned during the semester. They were also encouraged to give the teachers feedback regarding the pedagogy of Arts Seminar. The final exam for the course is shown in Figure 2.4.

In sum, the projects in Arts Seminar usually were in response to an overall question. There was usually a research component as well as a presentation-exhibition component that involved work in alternative media. And there was always an attempt to get students to reflect on the entire experience of creating and delivering the project.

THE MONUMENT PROJECT

During the 1998–99 school year, I observed the complete cycle of one assignment—the Monument Project—in Arts Seminar from the presentation of the concept on the first day to the exhibition of the final products. This is the project in the vignette at the beginning of this chapter. For the collaborative portion of the project, students were to create a three-dimensional abstract model of a monument commemorating a person, event, or a phenomenon. Students were given a sheet of paper with several abstract shapes on them, such as circles or triangles, and they were to use these shapes to design an abstract monument. Figure 2.5 shows the assignment sheet that was given to students.

Over 75 students were in the class that I observed during the 1998–99 school year. In interviews, students mentioned that they had signed up for the class because they had heard good things about it from older siblings or friends, or because they wanted to go on the New York City trip that was usually included in the course, or because they needed an arts credit on their transcripts. As an aside, the teachers mentioned to me that the class did not work as well together as had previous Arts Seminars classes.

The first step in the Monument Project was that students were to research other known monuments and keep a record of the research. Each student was to develop a philosophy about the shapes, colors, materials, arrangement, and size of monuments. Also at the beginning of the project, the concept of abstract communication was discussed. Students were asked to draw abstract shapes that express different human emotions (Edwards, 1987, 1989). Once this overview of abstraction was discussed, the students were then placed into groups to create a model of a monument for one person, event, or phenomenon. Once a subject was determined, each group was to propose three possible designs for their subject with one design ultimately being chosen by the group to be built and presented to the entire class.

The first day that the assignment was introduced, the class met in the choir room. Zasa began the class with a prior knowledge exercise. He asked students to break into groups and to think about the monuments they already were familiar with. Each group was given a large piece of chart paper and asked to list the things they knew about monuments. Students immediately broke into groups of two or three as Zasa, Peck, and Sentz walked around and talked to the groups as they worked. Most groups spread out on the floor at the various lev-

FIGURE 2.4 Arts Seminar Final Exam

Respond to the following:

The U.S. Congress is considering a bill that would eliminate all federal funding and support for the arts. Using what you have learned this year, write a letter to your congressman either supporting the bill or arguing why the congressman should vote
against it.

Project-Based Learning

You have just completed a course structured around project-based learning. Discuss
the following:

1. What are the strengths or advantages of this approach to learning?
2. What are the weaknesses or disadvantages of this approach?
3. What was the impact of time management on completing project work? (How
   easy or difficult was it to meet with group members?)
4. Can groups be constructed in a random manner? Why or why not?
5. Was the cost factor a consideration in the creation of project materials?
6. What suggestions can you make to improve the process?

---

els of the choir room where the choir would normally stand.

A group of three girls asked Peck, "What's that thing in St.
Louis?" "The Gateway Arch," Peck responded. He asked, "Do you
know who did it?" No one did. He answered, "Saarinen. Built it for
the World's Fair." The girls went on to list the Washington
Monument, the Lincoln Memorial, and the Statue of Liberty.

In another group, three girls wrote on their chart paper:
"Monuments represent something." Their paper was filled with pictures and fantastic printing. A girl in the group kept singing. "I feel
like singing," she said. Zasa spoke up to the whole class:
"Somewhere on your paper, give a definition of a monument." One
group wrote on their chart paper: "Tall, monochromatic, meaningful,
relate to historical events."

After a few minutes of this, Peck and Zasa asked students to call
out some of the monuments they listed on their chart papers. Peck
wrote the names on the board: Eiffel Tower, Mount Rushmore,
Vietnam Memorial, Arc de Triomphe, Iwo Jima Memorial,
Stonehenge, Free Stamp, Liberty Bell, Sphinx, biggest ball of twine,
Acropolis, Old Ironsides, flag on the moon, golden arches, Taj Mahal,
and Jefferson Memorial. There were also some comments about mon-

FIGURE 2.5 Monument Project Assignment Sheet

The Project

• Students will research other known monuments and keep a record of the
research. A diversity of types of monuments is desirable. Find out:
A. Who or what is the monument for?
B. Who designed it (if known)?
C. Where is it located?
D. Why does it look the way it does?
There should be at least one for each member in the group.

• Research the subject for your monument. Why is the person, event, or phenomenon important? What should we know about this person, event, or phenomenon
from your monument?
• Develop a philosophy about the shapes, colors, materials, arrangement, and size of
your monument. Why did you make the choices you made?

The Process

• After historical research of other monuments is done, the group will propose
three possible monument projects for approval.
• Research the subject.
• Design the monument and create the model using the shapes provided.
You may use only the shapes given—no additional shapes, but you may use them
as many times as you think you need to.
You may not make them smaller.
The shapes may be attached in any manner you like.
• Your written research and the oral presentation should answer the questions:
1. What is a monument?
2. Why is it made?
3. What should it look like? Why?
4. What does it tell?
5. Where should it be placed? Why?

Present and discuss your model.

uments that some students called out, including "dedicated to someone," "they're in significant places," and "relate to historical
events."

Zasa asked students to turn their own papers over and give a definition of a monument or give characteristics of a monument. "What
you're doing," he said, "is drawing conclusions." Peck then put an

overhead transparency on the screen that had the requirements for the Monument Project. The students began copying down the assignment. As the students copied, Peck outlined the assignment.

By the next time I visited, groups were working on their models. The groups were working in several art rooms that are close together in the art wing of the building. Peck, Zasa, and Sentz circulated between the rooms. In the planning period before the class, the teachers discussed their concerns that not enough of the models were being designed in an abstract fashion.

Peck, talking to one of the student groups, said,

> When you explain this [monument to the entire class], you're going to be explaining why you're choosing these [shapes]. . . . It's going to take you about 5 days [to make the model]. . . . You have to translate what you've drawn into a three-dimensional form. In a drawing, we often get one view. In a three-dimensional sculpture, people can approach it from any number of directions. It should be interesting from each direction.

During my time of observing the Monument Project, I followed the progress of two groups in particular—one that was working on a monument to Dr. Seuss and another that was working on a monument to Walt Disney. I tried to select a group that seemed to be doing well with the assignment (the Dr. Seuss group) and one that was perhaps struggling a little (the Walt Disney group).

Another reason I picked the Walt Disney group was because, during one of my observations, I overheard one of the group members saying that she hated this class. Another group member spoke up and said she loved this class. When I interviewed Debbie, she denied that such an exchange took place. Debbie did describe the progress of their group: "We wanted to do Jimmy Buffett, but they wouldn't let us, so we just thought Walt Disney would be easy and, so, we didn't want to do the work, so we just kind [of] like . . . [took the] easy way out." I asked how they had come up with their design for the Walt Disney monument. "Actually," replied Debbie, "the one girl, she had her own design, and we were going to do that, but she got really sick, so I made up the design, just 'cause we had nothing else to do, and they wouldn't let us sit there till she got back, so it was kind of like a spur-of-the-moment thing."

The finished Walt Disney monument consisted of some abstract shapes—a large sphere with two large microphone-shaped objects standing behind the sphere. But when viewed from a distance, the structure formed the outline of the head of Mickey Mouse. Also, the large sphere was supposed to stand for Epcot Center in Disney World. It could in no way be considered an abstract monument. Several other groups also seemed to struggle with expressing ideas abstractly. The Fred Astaire group, for example, designed a monument that was wholly figurative—a large top hat resting on its side. It looked like a float from the Macy's parade.

The group working on a monument to Dr. Seuss had originally wanted to design a monument that featured a figurative depiction of the Cat in the Hat. In a later interview, Peck described what he said to the group to try to get them back on track: "I said . . . if you use these shapes . . . to symbolize that kind of offbeat quality, then you achieve that sense of abstraction and it represents essentially what Seuss is about [more than a figurative drawing might]."

Gary, of the Dr. Seuss group elaborated on how their group came up with their abstract design:

The cylinders are painted different colors to represent his emotions and writing books. Like everybody has a dark side, so at the bottom of the spirals it symbolizes his dark emotions. As it goes up through the spiral, it indicates his lighter emotions, his happiness that he wanted to spread to his viewers.

Presentations

The culminating activity of the Monument Project was that each group presented its finished monument model to the entire class. First, each group presented some biographical information. Then, the meaning of the monument was explained. For some of the monuments, however, not much explaining needed to be done because they were created in a figurative manner. Most of the students paid attention and took notes on the presentations. It was clear that some groups were still having difficulty with the concept of abstraction. In a later interview, Peck expressed that perhaps the teachers shouldn't have allowed the class to build monuments to individuals, but rather to abstract concepts. "The project is not about a monument," he explains. "It's about abstraction. And we thought that having them create a monument form would give them a matrix on which to hang an abstract concept."

While the teachers expressed frustration that too many of the monuments had figurative elements (rather than being totally abstract), it was clear that this new literacies classroom did feature, at the very least, explicit discussions between students and teachers about the merits and disadvantages of abstract versus figurative means of communicating ideas. Even if not all students were capable of expressing themselves in an abstract manner, they had had the challenge of doing so laid before them in an explicit manner by the teachers. As Peck said, the project was about abstraction, not about some famous person.

WHAT THE STUDENTS SAY

There were many references to both learning and emotion in the interview transcripts from Peck, Zasa, Sentz, and their students and in the field notes from my observations of the class. What follows are some themes that emerged from the data.

Understanding of Content

Several students focused their comments more on what they learned about the person they were memorializing than on the principles of abstraction. Students were also able to make the distinction between these different goals of the project. Colin, a member of the Dr. Seuss group, mentioned that, while there wasn't a whole lot of "informational learning" from the Monument Project, there was a lot of learning about process—how to work with others. (Colin contradicted himself later in the interview, however, when he said that he did learn informational "stuff" in the course. He cited the project base of the course as one of the main reasons he learned content.) Colin came the closest to articulating the teachers' intent of the assignment: "I think I actually do have a better appreciation of art. Because, when I go to the museum, some things I can really sense. . . . I think that if I went now, that I would have a better sense of looking at it, realizing what the artist meant and did during that."

Gary said that he learned a lot about Picasso and the cubist painters. Debbie said she was glad that she signed up for the course because it's an "easy A" and because she needed the credit. But when I asked her to describe a class in her high school experience where she really learned something, she mentioned Arts Seminar. "Because all the other classes stick to basics and this is like a more . . . widespread, like a broad thing," she explained. When I asked Angie how she learned differently about Fred Astaire in a class like this, she responded, "You learn more about him, like just not the person, all the facts. You learn who he really is."

Understanding of Symbol Systems and Forms of Expression

Some students in Arts Seminar formed understandings of non-print forms of expression, some claiming that the course made them more "well rounded." Erin described her experience of being in this class: "I've learned . . . what colors mean and, . . . abstract meanings of things. . . . Now I see so much more than what I saw before." The experience informed Erin's writing by influencing her to use the "pictures you see in your head." Erin and some of the students reported having a sense that there are multiple forms of representation, and that these multiple forms are more accessible to them, both as readers and writers of these forms. As mentioned above, Peck would say things like, "You have to translate what you've drawn into a three-dimensional form." Even the fact that he was using the term "translate" with students and that they would have some concept of moving back and forth between print and nonprint media was evidence that the teachers were spotlighting that print is not the only form for reading and writing about Western civilization.

Fluency

In reaction to their ability to use forms other than print, it appeared that some students found a level of fluency they had never attained before. For these students, it was enabling to be free to communicate using alternative forms. The three teachers described one of their students who was extremely shy and had great difficulty communicating until he sat down at the piano. Peck remembered,

> To listen to him try to express himself with words was terrible. But he'd show you a picture or play a piano and it was all there. . . . I think that applies to a lot of kids. You know, sometimes they're just not given the opportunity to do some of these different kinds of things and to show what they're good at.

As Zasa pointed out, Arts Seminar may have been an oasis in a school day that does not always encourage fluency in alternative forms. In traditional classrooms, students are "told that if you're not verbal, then you're not intelligent," Zasa noted. "This [class] breaks that paradigm. . . . You are an intelligent person and . . . [you're] fluent in the way that [you] draw, the way that [you] use music."

Some students began to articulate a preference for certain symbol systems. During the fall of 1997, a student named Robert said,

> Art is a lot more visual, and I like to think with my eyes. Music seems more vague, because I'm not as involved in music. . . . If I look at my artwork, I don't think it's good at first, then . . . you gotta step back and look at the whole picture, and if you consider it for a while, it just starts to look good, you know? It's like, you can actually see the progress. Whereas, like, I don't know, I can't hear the progress as well.

Also in 1997, student Roger described words as being more "orthodox" and the "norm" in school: "Words, you can't get too far out there. I mean, with art, you can . . . the whole point of art is to build and create and make something, you know, visually, graphic . . . Every other class I . . . have deals with . . . words and writing reports and stuff." Students were able to draw a clear distinction between Arts Seminar and more traditional classes, and for many of them, being able to express themselves in nonprint media was freeing.

Collaboration

In the interviews, many students noted the collaborative nature of the class as what stood out. Barry almost apologized for liking the collaborative nature of the class, saying that he's not "shammin'" (lazy). He spoke of gaining from the perspectives of other people in his group. "Everybody is better at something than somebody," Angie stated, "so you may be better at one aspect of something, but somebody else can give you another idea." Angie also thought it was a better idea not to work always in the same group; she enjoyed working with a variety of people in the class. Debbie felt that she learned to depend on others. The amount of collaboration also teaches social skills, she said. Erin admitted, "I think it takes more to work in this kind of setting than to just sit there and listen to a teacher preach." Again, students noticed this collaborative element as a feature that set this class apart from their other classes in which they labored individually to memorize information for tests. Students felt that learning to collaborate with others was a skill that they had learned from the class apart from any Western civilization content.

Several of the students mentioned also benefiting from witnessing the collaboration of the three teachers of Arts Seminar. They spoke of getting different perspectives from each of them. Barry said, "You get more ideas, like . . . one teacher may say something the other teacher didn't say. It makes it easier to comprehend what they're trying to teach us."

Overall, students appreciated that Arts Seminar centered around projects that required some application of knowledge and that it was empowering and gave them a sense of ownership. Students also appreciated that the class was interdisciplinary and that it was collaborative, both for students and teachers. Many students also cited that the course was fun and engaging as reasons for their learning more.

PIONEERING STEPS OF ARTS SEMINAR

Arts Seminar was a class that matched the ideals of multiliteracies pedagogy described by C. Luke (2000)—depending "on viewing knowledge (and teaching) as integrated, thematic, multimodal, and interdisciplinary" (p. 435). However, I'm not convinced that the Arts Seminar teachers were going some steps beyond a "focus on whole language, process writing, and personal growth" (A. Luke, 2000, p. 451), to a "shift in educational focus from the 'self' to how texts work in contexts" (A. Luke, 2000, p. 453). Still, the assignments were always to place the various artists, musicians, and writers studied within the context of the artists' times, and by placing such an emphasis on living out the artistic process themselves, the implication was that students would empathize and even emulate the artistic process, not to mention the research process. As Zasa said, the teachers were trying to get at "the idea that the arts are a reflection of ourselves, and our culture, what that means."

While I was initially attracted to the class because of its relying on nonprint media to teach Western civilization content, as I listened to the students and observed their work, what began to strike me as the teachers' most significant accomplishment was that the class was using these alternative forms of communication to break down traditional models of pedagogy and to design a new space for learning content. In most high school Western civilization courses, the teacher might present the content in lockstep form, chronologically, in lecture format, with students' being assessed using multiple-choice and essay questions. Students would essentially be expected to memorize various important facts that would change sequentially from week to week. When the class was "done" with the ancient Greeks, they would move on to the Romans and so on.

In Arts Seminar, however, it was clear that students were able to cross boundaries of these rigid classifications of time and place as they also crossed boundaries of forms of representation. During the interviews with the students, I began to note the variety of text creators that were mentioned from a variety of media as well as time periods—Jackson Pollock, Alfred Hitchcock, Dr. Seuss, Mozart, Fred Astaire, Steven Spielberg, Emily Dickinson, Jim Henson, Walt Disney, Grand Master Flash, Steven Sondheim, Rembrandt, Sir Francis Bacon, Michel de Montaigne, Andrew Marvell, Beethoven, and Picasso. And students talked about absolutism, cubism, and abstract expressionism. These names and concepts were used in the context of their explaining to me what they had done in class. These students were not name-dropping. It appeared that they had learned the significance of these individuals and their perspectives. As Zasa suggested, the students seemed to learn more about these persons and their eras because they worked directly with these ideas in applied projects. Students were then able to go back and forth between centuries and artists, musicians, and writers as they discussed the "essential questions," translating from one form to another with an intertextual dexterity that may be as important as if not more so than the memorization of facts (C. Luke, 2003).

By focusing on questions and projects to be executed largely in nonprint media, the Arts Seminar teachers taught their students a new "grammar" (New London Group, 1996), and I'm not only speaking of the grammar of abstraction, although that was taught as well. I believe the teachers gave the students an entirely new way of approaching knowledge in the context of a new way of "doing school." This was not a simple endeavor, and if some students reacted by stating that the course was "easy," it may have been because they had never realized that learning could occur in a new space, disassociated with memorization of facts. It was significant that both teachers and students struggled with the understandings they were coming to as they worked with this new "grammar" and as the words *translate* and *design* became part of their everyday vocabulary. It could be argued that perhaps some of the students' and teachers' frustration could have been alleviated if the teachers had spent more time explicitly discussing the aim behind their assignments. Some of the Arts Seminar students may have been less frustrated by the monument assignment, for example, if the goals of the project had been more explicitly discussed. On the other hand, student frustration may not have been able to be avoided because students were not accustomed to learning in this manner. The students had been freed from the traditional memorization-of-facts paradigm that existed in the rest of their schooling; indeed, one of the projects assigned during the year was "What's it like being a student at Parma High?" Even though students did not come up with the essential questions in the class themselves, they had more freedom in this class to answer questions in their own ways than in any other class at Parma High.

Sometimes the teachers became frustrated. Peck lamented, "The project isn't about a monument! It's about abstraction!" However, Zasa noted, "Within the space of 15 minutes, you can hear them discussing the basic principles of abstraction. Without us ever having to have articulated for them what they were." If there were students who spent their time constructing figurative representations of Mickey Mouse's ears, I also witnessed students struggle (and sometimes fail) to conceptualize monuments that were abstract representations as well as intertextually connected to other artists, thinkers, and eras. "Everything has a connection," student Gary noted. "Like Beethoven was trying to illustrate something through his music. It was written down, which illustrates writing which is English. Some of the great tapestries probably were painted [to] his music."

What is without doubt is that these three Parma teachers demonstrated courage in the revitalizing of Arts Seminar. They were all veteran teachers either at the midpoint or end of their careers. It would have been very easy for them to coast through these years. Their courage to explore and enact a new literacies curriculum for this course was truly something to be celebrated.

Sadly, the revamped Arts Seminar lasted only for a few years. For economic reasons, in the spring of 2001, Arts Seminar was completely eliminated and is no longer offered at Parma High. As Peck wrote me in a recent email, "I retired in 2002, and Rich in the spring of 2003. All three of us agree that the best time we had in our teaching careers were the years we taught Arts Seminar together. The planets must have been lined up just right. I feel most fortunate to have been involved in this noble, if short-lived, experiment."

Chapter 3

DESIGNING SPACE IN A RURAL CLASSROOM

Profile: Clarence Fisher
Joseph Kerr School, Snow Lake, Manitoba

Snow Lake, Manitoba, Canada, is a future ghost town. The people who live there all know it. It is a fact of life for them. The town is completely dependent on a couple of nearby gold mines. As the mine goes, so goes the town. The nearby ghost town of Herb Lake closed down decades ago, and everyone knows this will eventually be the fate of Snow Lake. When I visited Snow Lake in the spring of 2003, there was increasing talk of the imminent shutdown of the mine due to a strengthening Canadian dollar, a lower grade ore, and the troubles of the mine's multinational parent corporation. Although the town is extremely remote geographically, it is inextricably tied to world events for its very survival. And thanks to the Internet and satellite television, the people of the town are now at long last media rich, more than at any time in their brief history, so much so that Clarence Fisher says, "Geography has become irrelevant." But has it really?

It was through the Internet that I found Clarence Fisher, a new literacies teacher who requires his students, among other things, to create websites focused on the now-ghostly town of Herb Lake—a town over which hovers the legendary presence of the lonely prospector Kate Rice, who lived by herself on two islands in the middle of Herb Lake and eventually went mad (Duncan, 1984).

THE SETTING

Snow Lake is a town of about 1,300 people in northern Manitoba. Manitoba is a central province of Canada with approximately one million people, about two-thirds of whom live in the capital city of Winnipeg. Most of Manitoba's 54 school districts enroll fewer than 2,500 students each (Levin & Wiens, 2003). Incomes are high in the town, because the mine pays well for the dangerous work involved with gold mining. However, the homes of the townspeople are relatively small, because people don't put very much money into homes that may become valueless literally overnight depending on the mine's fortunes, and because homes don't stand up very well in the relentless -40°F winters that the town experiences. Fisher says that the townsfolk put most of their money into "toys" such as "skiddos" (snowmobiles) and "quads" (four-wheel all-terrain vehicles).

Fisher summed up the local unease: "That's life in a small town. There used to be five operating mines in the area. And we had 500 kids at the school. [But] the mines have shut down, and we're now down to two operating mines. [Now] we only have 280 kids." The people in the town not only live with economic uncertainty, they live with physical danger on a daily basis. Signs hang outside the mine stating how long it has been since the last "lost time" accident. "When I was a teenager here, for about 5 or 6 years," Fisher said, "just about every year someone was killed in the mine. It's been a few years now since there has been someone killed."

It was surprising to encounter a new literacies classroom in an environment that, until recently, had been so media poor, particularly in terms of mass communication. There is no radio station in town, for example. As I made the 2-hour drive from the nearest town of Flin Flon (another mining town), I was able to pick up one radio station. The program that morning consisted of an announcer's calling bingo numbers. Apparently one could pick up the bingo cards at participating stores and play along with the radio. This went on for many minutes—"G8, G8, that's G8. [long pause] B4, B4, that's B4." Occasionally, the announcer would proclaim that this was Flin Flon's "Number one radio station," but even the announcer admitted that this was "Flin Flon's *only* radio station." "Daily" newspapers are delivered to the store a day late, because they are coming from Winnipeg, which is a 7-hour drive. There is no cell phone service in Snow Lake. Only recently has the town received 911 service. Until the 1970s, the television reception provided only one channel—the

Canadian Broadcasting Corporation (CBC). There has never been a movie theater in town. There is no video store, although one can rent from a small selection of videos/DVDs at the grocery store, where one finds the few videos on a shelf next to a freezer labeled "minnows."

In the last few years, however, the townspeople have experienced a virtual torrent of media choices with the advent of satellite dishes and internet access. Students report some frustration at the inefficiency of their home equipment—students have 56K dial-up internet service at home—but there are still many more media alternatives in the town than there were just a few years ago. It was partially this influx of media that prompted Fisher to examine what he was teaching in his self-contained classroom. Perhaps even more due to their remote isolation from the rest of Canada and the world, he wondered whether the students of Snow Lake would need some kind of crash course in new literacies.

AN AWARD-WINNING SCHOOL AND CLASSROOM

Clarence Fisher teaches in a self-contained (and therefore completely integrated) classroom at the Joseph H. Kerr School (http://www.jhk.mb.ca), a K–12 school with a total of 280 students. His self-contained configuration is not due to a district belief in curriculum integration, but rather due to the school's population size. Fisher is the only eighth-grade teacher for the 21 eighth-grade students in the school. The students are with Fisher all day, every day, and some of them have been with him before, as he taught them in lower grades as well.

Even though the school is small, Fisher has been able to garner several awards for himself and the school. Fisher was named a Manitoba Middle Years Outstanding Educator, and he and the school have been one of six Canadian members of the Grassroots Twin Schools Project team that traveled to the Netherlands to promote globalization of education. His Herb Lake project was named one of the top Grassroots projects in Manitoba. In 2001, the Kerr School was also named one of the Canadian Network of Innovative Schools by Industry Canada. This award is given to 30 schools a year that are shown to be innovative in the use of computer technology and daily assignments. The award came with a $30,000 grant that the school has used for professional development of teachers and for purchasing of equipment.

Fisher described how the school improved:

In 1998, staff at JHK school began to think deeply about the curriculum that we offer, the type of education students receive in our building, and about the skills they require to succeed in society. Based upon these discussions, which lasted the course of a year, our school undertook a program which we call Challenge, the "challenge" being to restructure our program to ensure that our students receive the most advanced education possible and that they have the skills they require to live in a twenty-first-century advanced society.

The Challenge program has five goals: implementing integrated, multidisciplinary units; emphasizing using technology in classrooms on a daily basis; emphasizing the use of higher level thinking skills in classrooms; establishing strong basic skills standards; and developing appropriate report cards. Fisher stated that, in reality, not all teachers in the school have used the multidisciplinary units, and that administrative turnover in the school district has led to the waning of interest on the part of some of the teachers. Still, the elements of a Challenge classroom exist in Fisher's classroom. It is obvious that Fisher pursues this kind of teaching because he is passionate about this kind of teaching himself. As he explains:

I guess how it started is I was doing my Master's at the University of Alberta, and I started running into a lot of information on, I guess it's called "textual grammar"—the idea that there's rules of text and that kids should know them. So I found that really interesting and the effects of some of the studies I'd read about how it increases comprehension levels in kids. So I started looking . . . at nonfiction. I mean if you take something in the social studies textbook, it looks really different from a novel, you know, so how do you start teaching kids rules about this stuff—that there's pictures, that there's timelines, that there's captions? And then, just as I started to get more interested in computers, it advanced into that.

At the same time, Fisher became concerned about keeping his students aware of potential manipulation by the media. "I started looking at web pages and started seeing the same ideas as a social studies textbook, only more advanced, with video, audio, text, pictures, all in one space, on one page, I mean never mind the advertising tucked in there as well! How do you teach kids to think about this stuff? How do you teach kids to know what's real and what's not?" Fisher said that he was influenced by the work of Paolo Freire, and by Klein's *No Logo* (2000), and saw his own students in Freire's descriptions of those he worked with: "I mean some of Freire's ideas—the Brazilian peasants—I mean that's what a lot of kids strike me as, 'cause they don't really understand what's happening around them."

From being concerned with students' abilities to read in different texts, Fisher made the jump to having his students compose in alternative texts as well:

> I guess the old saying [is] that the best way of learning something is by doing it. And so we started to move into the other idea of making kids producers, you know, of web pages, and short videos, of flash presentations . . . . You know, just the idea of presentation, of production, and that really seemed to strike at the idea of, you know—"Now I know how that's done!"

Central to Fisher's principles of teaching reading and writing is a nonhierarchical view of text. As with many of the teachers profiled in this study, Fisher always uses the word *text* when communicating with his students about print, music, video, or whatever text is being discussed. He also talks often with the students about texts being spaces.

> You know, especially when [we're] talking internet, I talk about an electronic space that's filled with either the written word, or video or audio or a picture or whatever that is. And we talk a lot about designing a space, you know, and that space can have anything in it. You know, it can be a Word document; it can be a PDF file, it can be an MP3.

Fisher traces his interest in space to the work of Canadian critic Northrup Frye:

> Northrup Frye says that the wilderness to people, the back country, is really one of the defining things of the Canadian psyche—just the idea of the unknown, the vast space, the blank space which we can escape to pour ourselves into. I guess I kind of connect it without thinking of it, cause I think of a web page as a blank space, and how are kids pouring themselves into that

space, you know, with all the different things they're able to . . . whether it's print text or video or animation or whatever? You know, how are they ordering that space? How are they designing that space to make meaning for themselves and make meaning for their audience? How do you live within your space? . . . And I guess I've also talked some about the idea of geography being irrelevant. So again, there's space.

Crossing and linking more spaces, Fisher described a project that he did last year with his students and some students in the Netherlands. To go along with a United Nations project on Sustainability, Fisher paired his students with those from a middle school in the Netherlands. The students were grouped across classrooms—each group had some students from Fisher's class and some students from the Netherlands class. Students were to research a local issue (such as water resources or transportation) and then post their notes in an allocated space using Knowledge Forum software (see Figure 3.1).

Fisher lamented that the project did not work out as well as he had hoped. The teachers in the Netherlands were using the project to assign a grade on how well their students used English, and this seemed to inhibit dialogue, except when students were at home. Once the Dutch students learned the home email addresses of some of the Snow Lake students, there ensued a lively personal exchange of emails, but the material posted on the official Knowledge Forum space was not of the quality that Fisher had hoped. When I asked a student named Melody about the Netherlands project at school, she said, "All we were doing was giving information that we already knew about our town, and we didn't get to interact with the Netherlands people. I mean, that was probably what the whole project was about, interacting with the people, but it didn't happen."

Another project closer to home that Fisher has done with his students involved the ghost town mentioned earlier, Herb Lake:

The kids had been studying the town itself for about 2 or 3 weeks. We had collected stories. We had written to people who used to live there and had old photos and things like that. And then when we got over there, . . . we had an original town map, and we had taken a lady with us who had lived over there, and she kind of pointed out where everything used to be first. . . . And then the kids split up . . . . We had two or three groups of kids, spread out through some of the trails that were still there. They went

**FIGURE 3.1 Internet Postings from the Joint Snow Lake–Netherlands
Project on Sustainability**

Our group is doing *agriculture*. The questions we are asking are:
1. What kinds of farming are to be found where?
2. What part of the working population is concerned with farming?
3. What is the average size of farms: (a) arable farming; (b) stock breeding?
4. What is being grown/cultivated?
5. How much milk is being produced?
6. How much meat is being produced?
7. What are the perspectives for the future and how are they being anticipated?

We are doing a project on *electricity* and how it is different in Haaksbergen,
Netherlands, and Snow Lake, Manitoba. We focused on only five main questions which
were:
• What is the annual usage of electricity by households and companies in Snow
   Lake and Haaksbergen?
• Where are the power stations that supply Snow Lake and Haaksbergen located?
• What are the different ways that electricity is generated in Snow Lake and
   Haaksbergen?
• Are environmentally safe ways of generating electricity being considered? If yes,
   why and in what way?
• What are the perspectives for the future, and how are they being anticipated?

We have completed a research project on *industries* in Snow Lake, Canada, and
Haaksbergen, Netherlands. The questions we were trying to answer were:
1. What kind of industrial companies can be found?
2. Where are industrial zones/sites located?
3. What factors make these locations especially suitable for industry?
4. What part of the working population is employed in industry?
5. What are the perspectives for the future, and how are they being anticipated?

We have completed a project on *neighborhoods and houses* in Snow Lake and
Haaksbergen. We have not uncovered many differences, and have learned that over
great distances, through different languages and cultures, people are still the same
underneath.

---

through with their digital cameras and video cameras, took pictures of some of the cabins that were falling down. You know,
they found a bunch of old canoes in the bush, you know, just the
artifacts that they could find from the town when it used to be
there. And . . . we went through the old mine that was there.

Students came back from the visit with ample digital photos and video and audio tape they had made, and they used much of this material to create a class website devoted to the ghost town of Herb Lake. The website stood as a witness space on the internet to a town that no longer exists.

THE ADVERTISING PROJECT

During the days that I visited Fisher's class in May 2003, his current eighth graders were busy designing their spaces according to the class assignment, which was to formulate a multimedia advertising campaign focusing on a product they had selected at random (see Figure 3.2 for the project assignment sheet). I found students were spread over several rooms in the school, with some in the computer lab working on Flash animation for their websites, some out in the hall recording a radio commercial into a laptop, and some in the classroom storyboarding. Prominently displayed in his classroom was a flow chart that read as follows:

> A text carries a message from one person to another:
> Reader,
> Watcher,
> Listener,
> Viewer
> (the people who use their skills to comprehend the message).

Fisher challenged his students ultimately to use multiple forms to represent the research they would do throughout the year. Fisher explained how the flow chart helped the class:

> We have been talking about the fact that information can be encoded in a number of symbol systems which all have rules that we agree on, and that they must consciously understand these rules, and call upon a known set of skills in order to fully comprehend the message that is being presented to them. . . . [The flow chart is] a simple beginning [of our] discussions. We find that we are often coming back to this diagram as we expand our classroom discussions.

Most mornings began, however, in Fisher's rather traditional-looking classroom, with the desks in rows. Fisher admitted that he usually doesn't have his student desks in rows, but this year's class of

eighth graders challenged him, and having the desks in rows seemed
to lessen discipline problems. (In fact, the only time I observed any
discipline problems were those times during the day when Fisher was
giving them announcements or when they were sitting in their rows
listening to him talk.) Students began the day with silent reading of
print texts (although Fisher says he is debating opening up this reading to other forms of texts). Then, after about 20 minutes, students
were generally "set loose" to work on multimedia projects. When I
asked Fisher what class or subject the Advertising Project was for, he
answered "English."

Fisher explained the rationale for the assignment:

> Information or entertainment is being pumped at [kids] from so
> many different channels. I think it can rapidly turn into a blur
> unless the kids have some critical structure in their brains to
> hang all of that on. And unless they have some time to sit down
> and physically separate this stuff in their head, and take a
> chance just to look in depth at something critically, I think it
> rapidly becomes just a corporate blur with no free space for kids
> to see something that's not corporate. And I think that's a big
> challenge with kids. They feel challenged by it themselves
> often. It's just so much and so fast and it's coming all the time.
> And I mean we're a long ways [from what] a lot of people take
> for granted. This is quite an isolated little place. And yet our
> kids still often feel that way.

By the time I arrived, the students were already well into their
advertising campaigns, but I could see evidence around the room of
some of the brainstorming that Fisher had done with his students at
the beginning of the unit. As Fisher described, they had started the
unit by looking at the characteristics of different ads and observing
trends in them. The list of brainstorming of general rules for each
type of ad was still hanging on the bulletin board. Under "Print,"
were the following characteristics: "Few colors, small, prices/deals,
description/info, good things big." Under "Television" were the following characteristics: "Speed (fast vs. slow), Pretty people, Music,
Colors fit the theme, POV (camera angle), Subtitles/narration."
Under "Internet" were the following characteristics: "Colorful,
Rectangular, Animated, Designed into page, Interactive games."
Finally, under "Magazine," were "Colorful, Big pictures, Large-sized
text, Design/technique, and Not much print." Now that students

FIGURE 3.2 Advertising Project Assignment Sheet

In this assignment, your group plays the part of an advertising company that has been approached by a client to design an ad campaign for their product. Your job is to design a campaign for print, audio/video, and the web.

Your client has given a deadline of June 13 for this campaign to begin (3 weeks) and only a very short extension (1 or 2 days) will even be considered. You must be prepared to work hard as a team to complete these ads on time to satisfy your client.

Here is the work outline:
1. *Audio / Video.* You must produce either a 25–35-second (no more, no less) television commercial or two 15-second radio ads. These ads must be well produced, including sets and costumes. For people considering a video commercial, you absolutely must be prepared to put in time at lunch and after school to learn to edit video. If you are not prepared to do that, don't consider this option.
2. *Print Ads.* Your client also wants a presence in magazines or newspapers. This includes either 4 newspaper ads or 3 magazine ads.
3. *Internet.* Finally, this client wants to be present on the web. They either want an online store designed, including a minimum of 5 linked webpages promoting their product, or 3 pop-up or banner ads produced using Flash.

Each of these products will be assessed individually and your group will be receiving one mark. As well, each group member will be evaluated several times throughout the work periods. At the end, each individual will receive the total of these marks as an individual work mark.

Every member of your group is expected to be working at all times. You cannot say, "X is doing the Flash part, so we're waiting until it's done." You can be planning your next ad or finishing up the one from before. Plenty of jobs need to be completed in this time, so manage your time wisely.

---

had been exposed to the ideas of Klein (2000), they were to design their own logos and their own complete avertising scheme for a product they had drawn at random. This ad campaign was to capture and persuade an audience through a variety of media.

On the project planning sheet (see Figure 3.3), it was interesting to see the emphasis placed on the process of carrying out the project. Students were being graded on their ability to create project timelines, divide up tasks, and stick to the plan. Fisher said:

They have full freedom for deciding where they're going to start, what they're going to do. They have timelines saying where approximately they think they will be, how they were going to build in their time, how they were going to build in the things they said they were going to build in—how to structure their ads, logos, colors, all those kinds of things. And how they were going to pull all these things together between all these different media. . . . So we talked a lot about structure. We talked a lot about evaluation being built in. The kids are all given rubrics with all the criteria. And then they're set loose.

STUDENTS AT WORK

The students' being set loose was exactly what I observed, as I saw work being done in various corners of the school. Some students were painstakingly assembling magazine ads from a combination of images found on the internet or drawn pictures that had been scanned in. Some were recording audio tracks and timing them to get them the exact length that they needed. Some were working on animation projects that would be woven into websites. Some were cropping and airbrushing pictures that they had found on the internet. All the students were extremely intent upon what they were doing. I think this was especially because they were coming off a couple days of not having access to the internet due to technical difficulties. It was particularly noticeable that some students who had been discipline problems in the traditional classroom setting were completely on task when set free to work on their advertisement projects. The students were just all quietly and intently going about their work, with the most laughter coming from the group that was creating the audio tracks for a radio ad. In fact, this group of boys were laughing hard as they recorded different tracks for their radio spot for skidoos. As one of the boys explained, "Well, our audio ads, we wrote them out, and then we have to tape them onto a computer. . . . And we just have to time it and get it right. Our print ads, we just draw on the computer. Our website is on the computer."

I asked the student what the difference was between creating a radio ad and an internet ad or a magazine ad. "Internet ads are all . . . there's lots to a page. Magazine ads, you just, you got like two to a page, and they're bigger and colorful."

"Each group has a different product they're trying to advertise," another student said. "We're advertising, like, skidoos, so we were making a new skidoo. It's called 'Unlimited.' And we have to make ads to make people want to buy it. So we were just kind of working on that."

FIGURE 3.3 Advertising Project Planning Sheet

1. Product _____
2. Brand Name _____
3. Five words you want the public to think when they see your product.
4. Who is the market for your product? How will your ad campaign appeal especially to this market?
5. What are the colors you are choosing for your ad campaign?
6. What do these colours have to do with your product?
7. Design a logo for your brand name.
8. How are you going to tie your campaign together (similar pictures, logos, colors, other)?
9. Design a timeline for your group. Make sure each member of your group has a copy and turn in a copy to Mr. Fisher. Your timeline should show quite specifically what each member of your group will be doing each day.
10. Turn in a second timeline showing what resources (video camera, computer lab time, other) you will be needing during each portion of your work. The school has limited resources, so we may not be able to get everything we need when required. Be prepared to change.

I asked him why their group chose to do a radio ad rather than a video ad. "Well, I think video is kind of hard," he said, "'cause you have to edit exactly what you say. 'Cause with radio, you just have to, like, you get a couple shots and you just say it, and when you're with video, you have to do it over and over, and then you have to splice it and edit. It's crazy." The boys had chosen a song by the rock group AC/DC for the background music for the ad. I asked why they had chosen such an old song, and Donald responded, "People identify more with that stuff. 'Cause your product is usually advertised to people over 18, if it's a skidoo, 'cause it's mostly those kind of people. So they'll remember AC/DC."

I also observed Teri, who was intent working in front of a monitor, using Corel Photopaint, attempting to assemble a magazine ad for a sports car, which was her product. I asked her about her ad campaign. "We're doing a video clip, and we're getting this guy—we're going out to the rock pit—and we're getting this guy to drive around and make donuts and stuff, and then there's going to be a song in the background. Haven't decided yet, but, yeah . . ."

When I asked Teri what she thought of this type of project, she answered,

It's more exciting and you learn more stuff, I think, because you're doing something you like to a certain extent and . . . I

don't know how to explain it . . . then you learn more stuff,
because you want to research it, so you can get a good mark on
your web page, so you can show everybody else. In writing,
you're just writing on paper and giving it to the teacher . . . .We
have a chance to see what the people who do those jobs, what
it's like for them to do their jobs.

I asked her whether she thought it was a waste of her time if she
ended up not being a professional web designer or advertising executive. "No," she answered, "even if you're working somewhere else
besides advertising, if you knew how to work the computer and
everything, it would still be good, instead of a waste of time." I asked
her if working on these ads has made a difference in the way she
shops. "Oh, yeah," she answered, "when I watch commercials, I
always try to figure out if they were done on video, or if they were
done on Flash animation."

Learning How to Use All Those Gadgets

Overall, when I asked students about their media lives outside of
school, they would typically say that they got on the internet (when
allowed) to chat on MSN. Donald admitted that he would sometimes
get on to find "cheats" for PlayStation 2. Another boy said he would
go to animation sites such as Homestar Runner (www.homestarrun-
ner.com) while other boys would play games such as WarCraft 3. One
boy said he would sell some of his Yu-Gi-Oh! cards on eBay.

I had to drag this kind of information out of the students, however. When I could get the students away from their work, they
weren't all that interested in talking to me. I found that they became
very quiet. Many students were barely, if at all, able to articulate the
purpose behind many of Fisher's assignments. If they were at all able
to articulate a reason behind them, it was frequently that learning
this technology would prepare them to better be able to get a job and
succeed on that job. A typical response to my question of what they
thought of learning these new literacies, was Chloe's: "Now we know
how to use all those gadgets—Flash. We can make everything on
Macromedia Flash; we could make, PowerPoint presentations, like,
massive presentations, we know how to do all this digital stuff. I
think I've learned a lot from that."

"Why do you think that's important?" I asked.

"'Cause our society's changing a lot," Chloe answered. "And

we're going to have to know how to do this stuff eventually to get a job and keep it and stuff like that. Technology is advancing a lot. We talk a lot about that in our classroom—technology."

When I asked what it is they learn from this kind of teaching, not a single student spontaneously generated "being aware of media manipulation" or a similar answer. Still, when I would ask a question such as "Do you find you watch television differently after doing this assignment?" they would invariably say yes. But what they would go on to describe about their viewing was mainly at the structural level—that they had actually timed a commercial to see if it was 30 seconds in length, for example, or that they had noticed the type of animation used in commercials. When I asked Chloe what she had learned from the advertising unit, one of the things she mentioned was about logos:

> We talked about all the logos. Like Nike is the big swoosh; as soon as you see it, it's well known. A lot of the well-known brands are like that. You see the logo, and you know what it is. We talked about blue being a really respectable color, . . . like the banks, they have blue. But . . . colors that you wouldn't really think of a logo in are browns, dark greens, and black. Not very good colors for a logo. You want to catch their attention. And it's very flashy, sort of.

Yet, when I asked Chloe whether this knowledge has changed the way she shopped, she answered that it has made her actually seek out those logos and purchase "good brand names" such as Nike. "I buy a good brand name of clothes," she said. "Like, if people are wearing them and they say that they're good high-quality clothes, you don't want them to fade. So yeah, I buy clothes with good brand names, like high-known, like Nike."

When I mentioned to Fisher that his students didn't seem to get the political dynamic behind the advertisement unit, he responded: "Part of it is that they're so immersed in it that there's really no way out. They don't really know how surrounded they are. And I think that's probably true of most North Americans." In a later email to me, Fisher also added that their answers to this question may have reflected their relatively young age. Overall, students didn't generate "media manipulation" when asked what they learned from Fisher's assignments. But there was no doubt that they saw the career benefits from doing the work, and they mostly found the projects to be fun and engaging.

It's Fun, But What Are They Learning?

While students saw Fisher's classroom as much more involving than other classrooms were, there seemed to be a split opinion from students as to whether they were learning as much in his class as in more traditionally taught classes. One girl stated that they "didn't get as much done" this year as they had with previous teachers and that they didn't have as much homework this year as before. Yet, many students reported working at home or after school for many hours to complete Fisher's assignments. It would be interesting to count the hours, in fact, to see if there were more hours worked at home in previous years when students had more traditional assignments. Regardless of number of hours, however, some students felt that what they were really learning with Mr. Fisher was how to use the technology, and that this was a good thing, to prepare them for the job market and to make the class "less boring." Certainly, the students seemed extremely engrossed in their work when they were working on these new literacies projects. It was clear that when they were working on more traditional projects the days that I was there, their interest waned.

This wasn't the first new literacies classroom in which I felt a tension between the goals of the teacher and the goals of the official curriculum and the goals of the students, although certainly one could point to many objectives in the Western Canada Protocol (the official curriculum) that would justify each element of the advertising unit that I witnessed. Still, there seemed to be a nagging doubt among some of the students that they were getting as much work done this year and about whether the skills they were learning were simply to be learned so they could be more attractive in the job market. Were students being sidetracked from a traditional English curriculum by Fisher's plan to have them learn how to do Flash animation during English class? And what of Fisher's goal to get kids to read and write critically in these new literacies, to be able to deconstruct and construct messages? Were these lessons being learned by the students, and if not, why not?

One partial answer came toward the end of my stay at Joseph Kerr School when I began to see some of the finished advertisement campaigns, designed by the students. I began to notice that almost each one of them had some element of parody, even though this was not part of the assignment. Whether it was the overblown hucksterism of the radio announcer selling skidoos expertly mimicked by the group of boys, or the apt knockoff of an Abercrombie and Fitch ad executed by a group of girls, the students were commenting wryly on the tried-and-true conventions of typical advertising. Two girls worked on an ad campaign for wearable paper bags that would protect the wearer from SARS. "And they're edible," said the one student who was working to assemble a representation of the paper bag by taking bits of different photographs she had found on the internet. "Plus, it helps you if you have to hyperventilate," said her partner, as she laughed.

The Abercrombie girls were doing a satirical ad that focused on sweaters that supposedly would not get dirty no matter how much dirt they came in contact with. The girls had staged a photo shoot with themselves out near the edge of Snow Lake. They had purposefully smeared mud and dirt over some old clothes they were wearing. Then, at the last moment before the picture was taken, they put a clean sweater on over their dirty clothes, so that it looked as if the sweater had deflected dirt while the rest of the clothes they were wearing attracted filth. The resulting pictures looked like a typical teen clothing ad, with the requisite studied casual poses out on location. Except for the fact that the girls were mostly covered with mud.

Perhaps it was in the students' parodies that students tacitly acknowledged the genres and designs and conventions of advertisers and how advertisers attempt to position viewers. Even if students were not very willing to explicitly discuss critical media literacy, their parodies stood without comment, effectively witnessing their acknowledgement of being positioned by the media, and even their own complicity in that positioning both as readers and now as writers of new literacies. Why should they have to state the obvious in words to me—an outside visitor to their world?

And it was clear that they were used to collaborating on these literacy projects, and it was good that they seemed adept at this, given that essentially these same 21 students had been together for the past 7 years and would be together essentially for the next 4 years. Fisher's most valuable work may have been this fostering of a social literacy, for it was during these assignments that the students seemed the most collaborative and engaged. This collaboration was probably healthy for a population who, due to the weather and the isolation of the town, spent much of the time alone, or with just a few family members. On the other hand, these students who worked together often played together in the evening, with daylight stretching during this time of year until 10:30 P.M. and even later. The students would go from a day of being together at school to an evening of fishing, or swimming, or playing baseball.

As I made the 2-hour drive back to Flin Flon where I would catch the small plane to Winnipeg, I thought about the new literacies I had seen in what is the equivalent of a modern one-room schoolhouse. I also thought of the lonely image of the mad prospector Kate Rice, living alone on the island in the middle of Herb Lake, staking her claim in silence. Suddenly, I looked out the window and saw a bear several hundred feet away, standing by the road looking back at me.

So is geography irrelevant? It seemed, at least in school anyway, that it was in the hybrid spaces they were able to design and fill up, that Fisher's students were the most free.

Chapter 4

"A Dot-Com with Salsa"

Profile: Marco Torres and Veronica Marek
San Fernando High School, San Fernando, California

On my way up the 405 (San Diego) Freeway north from the Los
Angeles International Airport, I saw exit signs for locations that
have become famous all over the world: Sunset Boulevard, Beverly
Hills, Century City (home of Twentieth Century Fox), and
Mulholland Drive. But when I got to San Fernando High School and
talked to the students of the San Fernando Education Technology
Team (SFETT) many of them said they weren't that interested in
getting into show business. They were more interested in becoming teachers. One student said, "I just do this because I love it."

Marco Torres and his teaching partner, Veronica Marek, were
nominated for my study by the George Lucas Education
Foundation (GLEF). In fact, Torres was the first teacher mentioned
by GLEF and is, in fact, the most "famous" teacher I studied for
this book. Torres is an Apple Distinguished Educator and has given
inservices and presentations all over the United States. In his relatively short 6 years as a teacher at San Fernando High School, he
has transformed an old shop classroom into a state-of-the-art New
Media Center and his students have met Steve Jobs of Apple
Computers, Spike Lee, and photographer Howard Bingham. Some
of Torres's students have gone on to become Apple employees,
traveling the country talking to teachers about technology.

But when I spent 2 days at the school and witnessed the school's
fourth annual "ican Film Festival," it was very clear that the students
were more impressed with what they could give back to their community than they were with any of the famous people they've met or
with any of the gadgets they have at their disposal. Even though stu-

dent Rosa had once visited the set of *ER*, she seemed more excited about coming back to the community to give back to the next generation of students. One of the things she wants to give back is the new literacies curriculum created by Marco Torres, although when I used the terms *new literacies* and *multiliteracies*, neither Torres nor his students had heard of them. When asked what inspired Torres to teach new literacies, he responded that he still remembers the volcano he made in third grade and that "technology is not just a tool; it is a part of our lives."

What Torres and Marek and their students have created at San Fernando High School has come to be known as the San Fernando Educational Technology Team (SFETT). This new media project has become integrated with the life of the school in several ways: as the home of a vibrant after-school program that culminates in a yearly film festival; as a site of various computer classes; and as a space for doing multimedia projects as assigned by content teachers in the school. All of this activity takes place in a transformed electronics shop room, now filled to the brim with new technologies. But it was clear during my visit that Torres feels it is not the technology, but the planning process he has put in place that empowers his students. In fact, he criticized schools of education for being focused more on pedagogy revolving around products than pedagogy revolving around process. It is the planning process, said Torres, that empowers the students to express themselves in any medium. It all begins with planning. Whether they are making a web page or a video, the students are expected to become slaves to the storyboard. They are not allowed to get near the technology until the storyboarding and planning process has been completed and approved by Torres or Marek. During the time I was there, I heard more about the planning process than I did about the content of what was being studied or produced. Indeed, sometimes it wasn't clear to me what I was observing—was this a social studies class, a computer class, an after-school club, or a start-up business ("a dot-com with salsa," as Torres called it)? I came to see that SFETT was all of these, but it went beyond any name that could be articulated—what students could articulate was that being involved with this creative team of students and teachers has been, for many, a life-altering experience.

THE SCHOOL AND THE TEACHERS

San Fernando High School, in San Fernando City, is on a campus so large that when I appeared at the main office, the secretary had to look on a chart to see who Marco Torres was and whether he was currently "on track" (the school operates on a year-round basis, with some students and teachers always on vacation, or "off track," so as to ease overcrowding.) This 9–12 high school, famous also for being the alma mater of Richie Valens and the site of some of the filming of the movie of his life, *La Bamba* (Valdez, 1987), contains 5,000 students and 238 teachers and is part of the Los Angeles Unified School District.

Eventually, the secretary found the room where Torres was supposed to be and directed me to an open hallway that was really an open-air walkway that connected all of the various buildings on the campus. There was trash lining the walkway, and the doors looked like the doors on prison cells. But when I opened the door to room 307, I was stepping into another world, a kind of new literacies oasis carved out of an old classroom.

Marco Torres was an engineering major at the University of California at Berkeley, who later attended the JFK School of Public Policy at Harvard, but did not enjoy his experience there. He decided to work for a city councilman in San Fernando City, but eventually took a leave of absence to teach in the Los Angeles Unified School District. As he described it, almost from the beginning, he had a plan to go beyond typical classroom teaching. First, he started going to a computer lab at an elementary and middle school on Saturdays and teaching computer classes in Spanish to some 300 parents. This was part of a strategy to build an advocacy parent group for technology. "In a poor school, the teachers rule; in a rich school, the parents rule," Torres explained. At these community events, Torres showed videos on how communities could obtain available federal dollars; he also used pictures and graphics to explain why it was their neighborhoods that ended up collecting 80% of the city's trash. From the beginning, he used mainly visual tools to communicate with his audiences and to build community awareness. He taught in this manner, he said, because, "I think in moving pictures. . . . I'm a visual learner because of language barriers. . . . Teachers traditionally haven't learned in these ways."

Originally hired to teach social studies, Torres would assign students to investigate the politics of lobbying organizations, for example. Students would be required to study a group such as Doctors Without Borders, form essential questions about such a group, and then give presentations culminating in the question, How can we get involved now? In another assignment related to economics, the students were to go to stores in their neighborhoods and attempt to buy a computer disk or a blank CD. The failure of the students to find retail outlets in their communities that sold such technology items made an impact on the students and also on local media, which covered the story. Torres stated that his goal was always to assign interactive projects; he wanted to influence politics, not just "do hyperstacks on the Pythagorean theorem." Here was a teacher, then, who was unapologetic about not necessarily tying all of his projects to the content of the curriculum, or, at the very least, he went beyond the social studies curriculum to immediately look for some interaction with the community. Torres, however, would go even further beyond the social studies curriculum.

THE CREATION OF THE EDUCATION TECHNOLOGY TEAM

The next step came from a student. Veronica Marek, an English teacher who has worked closely with Torres, explained:

> One of our students, Ernesto Hernandez, had the opportunity when he was a senior to be in a film with Jimmy Smits, called *The Price of Glory* (Avila, 2000). [As] he shot this movie, he realized that there weren't a lot of Latinos in front of the camera, and there weren't a lot of them behind the camera. And so what he decided to do was to come back and start a film festival.

From these roots, the ican Film Festival has come to be one of the main components of SFETT since 1999 when the first one was held. While the festival originally served as a venue for exhibiting student projects to the community, it has become over the years a vehicle for transcending the boundaries of the school, providing a yearly celebration of local people, both young and old alike. The festival also serves to help students transcend their traditionally passive roles, since students are responsible for organizing and administering every detail of the event, from shooting, editing, and burning copies of videos, to manning concession stands, to setting up chairs and publicizing the event. The festival that I observed, in July 2003, did not even take place at the school, but in an open-air courtyard donated for the evening by a coffee shop.

But former students remember that SFETT and the ican Film Festival started in a much smaller space with much less equipment than they have now. Former students Connie and Rosa reminisced that they started with computers that could only do a little animation, with AppleWorks and PhotoShop. "We only had five iMacs," remembered Connie, "and then we had Torres's laptop as well. But it's hard! At that time, everyone wanted to do their project." "Everyone was huddled around," said Rosa. "They had the little schedules to see who was going to do what." The equipment was not only being used to create multimedia projects for the film festival; it was increasingly being used by students to work on projects they would turn in for credit in content area classes.

More space was needed for the growing program, and Marco explained the institutional barriers that they had to overcome:

> My school is considered a failing school because of the percentage of kids that pass [standardized tests]. Eighty percent of kids of this age do better than they do. . . . Most kids will tell you we built our classroom in spite of the school demands. . . . I convinced the parents that test scores are basically based solely for school reputations. They don't do anything to develop human spirit in children. They don't do anything to support educators and make them feel better about the jobs that they do, and, most importantly, kids, especially here in my community, a lot of them have very low self-esteem. So, if I can make them feel good, make them feel special, then the parents feel good, and the parents feel special. . . . That is very rewarding and those little quick victories in their lives, builds will for them to make bigger decisions.

Even Torres's teaching credentials became an issue as he fought to find and remodel a classroom for SFETT. Torres related:

> I lost my job for 8 weeks 'cause I didn't have a credential to teach this. You know, I was a social studies teacher [and] this is a way for kids to understand, to study their social surroundings, and to make sense of their social surroundings, and to create opinions, and create stories and to share their stories in their social surroundings, so in the future, kids from this community could study the social reality that our kids here experience.

Yet, apparently, the fact that Torres was continuing to spend so much time teaching what was perceived as computer skills became a controversy within the school district. "So, you know what, the way that I look at it, it's a risk," Torres said. "I take a risk all the time. But mostly it's kids. We'll do it after-school, even if I was totally restricted, because this makes sense."

Not only were Torres's teaching credentials a problem, it was also a problem to obtain the size room that Torres and Marek wanted for transforming into a media studio. Finally, the teachers and students found an old electronics shop within the classroom that was being used for storage and occasional classes. Using donations and grants, Torres and Marek were able to put together the financing for the complete gutting and remodeling of the room. To design the new space, Torres and Marek got help from Norstan who flew the teachers to Arizona to see some of the media communication labs they had designed at schools. "We contracted with Norstan," Marek said. "They sat and listened to what we wanted and helped us out. We had a Digital High School grant, and then Norstan . . . pitched in. . . . Title I helped with purchases of the computers. We had donations from various people." The room was beginning to take shape as were the teaching philosophies of Torres and Marek.

ELEMENTS OF SFETT

Although Torres doesn't trace his philosophy of teaching to New Literacy Studies or to other writings on new literacies, it was clear that there were several elements of his classroom that resonated with much of those writings.

Physical Space

The room's feel and look was very important to the teachers. When one enters the room, there is quite a transition from the bright sunlight and noise to what feels like the humming deck of the Starship Enterprise. The darkened room is lit only by the glow of 40 computer terminals arranged in circles in groups of 8 in the center of the room. Along the walls are several small glassed-in rooms including a small music suite with a couple of electronic keyboards for adding music to videos; a "green room," with walls painted entirely in green to assist in creating video effects (similar to the green or blue screens that weather forecasters stand before); a conference room with video conferencing capabilities and a large bulletin board filled with storyboard sheets. There is also an office for SFETT and a couple of "think rooms" equipped with a desk and computer, and two very comfortable couches nearby. The entire room is dwarfed by a huge screen that is about 30 feet tall.

Marek explained that the teachers saw many computer labs in

schools in which the computers were sitting on tables facing walls or in rows. For the design of the SFETT new media lab, Marek related that she and Torres wanted their computers placed in groups. She explained, "We wanted to have little spaces where kids could meet and collaborate and just talk about projects. So we have these little 'think rooms' on the side. A lot of times when they're in the planning phase, a group of kids will go in there away from the larger group and work. They meet a lot of times in the conference room also." When I observed, the room had a buzz of activity with students intently staring at computers and stopping occasionally to consult with another student. Part of the intensity was that students were trying to finish their videos for the ican Film Festival which was only a few days away at the time of my visit. I also saw standard computer classes (PowerPoint, word processing) being taught by another teacher while I was there.

It was crucial to Torres and Marek that the equipment in the room be of professional quality, whether it is related to making music, or nonlinear editing, or animation. "We don't dummy down," said Marek. And Marek reported that the room has had no problems with graffiti or vandalism:

> The room has stayed looking really nice because [students] appreciate being in a clean environment. You go into our other classrooms, you'll see three different types of desks in the room. . . . [In this room] they sit in the chairs and the chairs give a little, and they really respect all of that. I think it makes a huge difference. Marco and I really wanted a nice place for our students. We wanted the best for them. And we wanted an environment where they could get some serious work done, and feel comfortable. It doesn't look like a classroom.

Process over Product

Students come to the new media lab via several different paths. They may have been brought to the lab by one of their content area teachers to work on a project. Or they may have signed up for the course, Computer Graphics, that is taught by Torres. (As mentioned, Torres has also been a social studies teacher at the school and has used the lab in that capacity.) However, the lines were so blurry between kids who were in the computer graphics class or kids who were in a content area class, or even between kids who were graduates or current students, that I finally quit asking them questions such as "How are you being graded on this?" or "What class are you in?" Those kinds of questions were obviously irrelevant to the students who were working in this kind of noncompartmentalized, interdisciplinary, in some cases nongraded space. Adding to the murkiness was the fact that the school operates on a year-round schedule, so at any time some students were "off track"—each student is on a different track, going to school for 4 months and then having 2 months off. Many students come in to the new media lab to make videos and other multimedia products during their 2 months off. So when one looks out over the lab, some of the students who are present may technically be on vacation. But such curriculum and calendar divisions are meaningless to the students who are drawn to what SFETT provides whether or not they are "on track," and whether or not they are being assigned some kind of credit.

A former student named Rosa explained how she originally got involved with SFETT:

> I had a Spanish class, and we had a little presentation to do, on like an artist or like a scene or some kind of performer. . . . so our teacher took us up there, and I was just, like, amazed with the room. 'Cause you walk in other classrooms, you know, they have desks and books, and things like that, you know, just completely different. You know, different color from every other room. It had a huge screen. . . . It's just too cool. . . . I was a sophomore at the time. And I walked in, and saw them working on projects, and we had cameras and all these cool things. I was just kind of hiding, . . .and then I talked to Torres and I had just asked what are they doing, "Oh, they're working on this project. They're doing this movie." They actually pulled me in to act in it—they needed someone. I just happened to walk in at the right time, and then I just kept going. . . . I just never left.

I was made to feel sure, however, that for those students who were "on track," (not on vacation) there were grades being assigned, and that the grades were based on how students completed the process of creating, more than on the end product. Regardless of what path the students use to enter the lab, what is paramount in Torres's teaching is the process of how one approaches a project. As Marek said,

> We started using this technology, but it's not really the technology we stress as much as teamwork, leadership, collaboration,

thinking, critically evaluating what they're doing. So it's like all these other skills are what the kids really learn to do. And the technology was really just on the side.

Rosa echoed the benefits of following this planning process:

> Personally, for me, I just think it's so much easier. . . . You know who's doing what—who's going to be your editor, who's going filming that you know, who's going to be there at what time, what time can we use this. It's just, you know, instead of like spending like 2 weeks on a movie, you can finish it, like, in 2 days. So I just think it's more efficient.

Collaboration is essential to this process. Torres and Marek have a rule that, if a student becomes confused, he or she must ask at least three other students for help before coming to a teacher. Marek explained that many of the students, when they enter SFETT, have difficulty communicating: "Even just saying, 'Hi,' is something that they're not accustomed to doing when they come into their class-rooms. . . . So what we do is we try to encourage students to collabo-rate, to work together, to think, to problem solve, to evaluate. And, um, the technology is just part of it."

The project, whether it's designing a website, or a Flash anima-tion, or a fully edited video, culminates with a presentation of the end product to the entire class. Marek described how students may begin with a simple animation in Appleworks—they draw, then take a snapshot, and put it together in Final Cut and add sound, credits, and a title. Once the project is done, she said,

> We have the kids . . . get up and present, and they have to explain, you know, what were their challenges. What did they like about the project? What would they do differently? And then they show it, and we always have a rubric where the class evaluates it, and then they give feedback, you know. You know—"This is really great about it, but did you think about doing this instead?"

Miguel described the peer evaluation process: "We don't just say 'It sucked. It's boring.' We [say], 'If it doesn't work, tell me why it doesn't work.' It's because how can I make it better? 'Your song is a bit too loud, it doesn't let the actor speak his mind.' That's the whole process of filming we use."

Torres spoke of encouraging the students to embrace failure: "We embrace failure and success equally here. You know, for almost every minute of production that they do, there's about a hundred minutes of things that did not succeed. . . . When they're learning something new they're not scared of that failure like most kids in schools."

Social Justice

Something that is immediately noticeable is that the students in SFETT are not interested in doing skateboard movies or slasher films. There is a passion about social justice that is never far below the surface. As Torres explained, those in the American civil rights movement have generally given a lot of credit to the help that images supplied the movement, in that it was the images (rather than print descriptions) of vicious guard dogs attacking African Americans, for example, that finally opened white America's eyes. Still, Torres pointed out, at least African Americans could and did make their own films; Latinos, on the other hand, "are always seen as an outside, nomad group that is going to leave." Even the media portrayal of the San Fernando Valley has been slanted toward the "valley girl" of Burbank and Sherman Oaks, and away from Pacoima, Sylmar, Lake New Terrace, and Sun Valley, which are the original towns in which Native Americans lived and to which the missionaries first came.

Most of the student multimedia projects I observed did have some message related to social justice. Connie, who is now majoring in linguistics and minoring in education at University of California at Los Angeles, explained the genesis of the video that she made about local sweatshops when she was a senior at San Fernando High:

> In our community, we actually don't have much of a voice, being that we are Latinos. That's pretty hard. So . . . I made a project on sweatshops. I never used Final Cut before, but I did know I wanted to do something on sweatshops, and I wanted to do it as soon as I could, just 'cause I had a feeling for it. And so Torres showed me two things on it—just text and pictures—and that's what I used to make it. So it was more like—what was it that I wanted to do with it, what did I want to use, because obviously I didn't have footage for it. The idea just came to me and I had information. . . . There's actually sweatshops in our community. I know it's ridiculous, but I mean, . . . it's kind of like quiet, silent, so we don't . . . we don't know about it until we actually tell everyone else.

When I asked Connie how she knew about the sweatshops, she said that she found out from her brother who would march in protest of the local sweatshops. "It's not only in Mexico or Indonesia," she said. "It's here." The resulting video is a powerful telling of that story—simply a series of pictures intercut with text. Connie was pleased that her message went beyond the teacher to whom she turned the video in for a grade:

> We have our own personal stories, and we have messages, and we have things that we learn, and we want to make sure that we're not the only ones that learn it. We want to make sure that, if we write an essay about it, it doesn't just go to the teacher, it actually not only goes to the classroom, but it goes worldwide. . . . We don't want to be shut down, we don't want to be quiet anymore. And now with the technology, that's just a special tool in order for us to get our voice heard.

Miguel confirmed this: "When I show them a movie, I'm showing them a piece of me. I'm showing them, this is what I want to say, but I can't so I'm going to let moving images do the talking for me."

I asked the mundane "teacher" question: "How were you graded on your sweatshop video?" Connie respectfully answered:

> I used my project for two different classes. . . . I used it for my economics class, and I used it for my computer graphics class. So I used the project twice. Not only did I do it for the class, though, I did it for myself. But, you know, it did work out for both classes. The way we do get graded on is: One, is your message heard? Did you tell it thoroughly? Was it objective or subjective? Did you get your point across? Can you hear the sound? Is it related to the topic that you're talking about in economics?

But it was clear that the grade that Connie received was the least of her concern as compared to the way the video itself has been received by outsiders. She reported that her video has been seen in China and Australia and had been shown by Steve Jobs, CEO of Apple, as an example of how technology tools can be used to give voice to students. Connie said, "So it's just like, wow, a little project that I . . . I thought it was little turned out to be a big thing, and now I inspired other kids to do it. . . . That's the key for me is that we can inspire other people."

Media Literacy Skills

Along with composing in video, music, PowerPoint and other presentational media, as well as animation, students also speak to how working with SFETT has made them better readers of media. Miguel said that he watches films twice now—the first time watching the shots the director and editor have chosen, the second time paying attention to the story. "The program made me into a whole other person. . . . It's kind of cool. Now I see television differently. Now I see a lot more."

When I asked Miguel how he learned all this, he answered, "Torres taught me every time you look at a frame, look at every possible angle there is. Why is there a light on his face? . . . There's a reason why they use close-up, so the audience will know. . . . There's a reason why they use specific shots for specific emotions." Jonathan spoke of being able to critique media technology analysts, saying that he was upset to hear someone on television speaking poorly of Canon XL-1 digital video camcorders which are the cameras used by SFETT.

Family Atmosphere

The students that I met seemed to enjoy expressing themselves and their own individuality, yet they balanced this individual creative expression with a true collaborative, family spirit. Even though many of the students have been successful individually, many of them ultimately want to come back to the family they've created here. Marek reports that many of their graduates come back on breaks to mentor current students: "It's very much a family feel to it, you know. We have parties together. It's members from 4 years ago, 5 years ago to the current students, and they'll help each other out. And these students that come back are always amazed at what the kids now are learning, what they're doing."

Connie agreed: "It's weird—I graduated 2 years ago. . . . There are people who graduated 4 years ago. We still come back together, during our vacation time, and that's one of our other goals—we want to always stay a family, and we always want to be working together. That's the goal." Miguel said, "I call it my digital family. Torres is my digital pops."

Learning Content

The students also spoke highly of how much content they had learned during their time with SFETT. Rosa stated that part of this learning might be due to the process of working on multimedia projects: "You see it over and over; you spend time editing and just it becomes really personalized. You spend all these hours, I mean. . . . researching all the information, planning the whole project, and actually putting all the text and the pictures and the video and the sound, so you have all those to appeal to all people, you know?" Torres reflected that his own school learning was mainly visually based: "I needed learning to be very visual, and I loved movies and I loved what movies can do. My mother was a photographer. A large part of what we do is based on our past. To not only see the images, but to be able to use them." As I mentioned earlier, it was difficult as an outside observer to pick apart what content was being taught during the time I observed in the new media lab. What was clear, however, was that students were not spending time making skateboard or slasher films. These media productions were filled with the passions of their makers.

SHOWTIME: THE ICAN FILM FESTIVAL

As the audience filled the chairs that had been set in the courtyard of a coffee shop, the students were upstairs in the SFETT Pro office, hurriedly burning the final DVDs that would be used to project the videos on the two big screens. What was impressive is that the students were doing all the work. Torres and Marek were simply observers. Occasionally, the teachers might be consulted by a student about something, but the students were running everything, from the assembly of the final DVDs to the selling of ican Festival T-shirts downstairs. Some of the students took time, in the midst of this organized chaos, to tell me about their dreams for SFETT Pro, a company which they hope will extend the work they have done with SFETT at school even further out into the community. Rosa explained, "SFETT Pro is pretty much an extension of SFETT . . . . SFETT still exists here, but once we left, the graduates like Connie and myself and some of the other people, still we always come around. . . . We just come back, 'cause we love the stuff we do here. We just decided, that like, why not make it a company?" The office of SFETT Pro is above the coffee shop, and the goal of the business is to offer such services as video editing and website design to companies, schools, and small nonprofit organizations in the community. Former student George added, "A lot of schools are looking for programs like this so they hire us to work [it] out and we work with their staff or their students. . . . We take some of the skills that we learn at the high school and we apply them."

"You know," said Rosa, "our parents, like people in our community, can't afford these outrageous prices for videos, [or] you know, if
you have a little shop and you want to put up a website. . . . So the
whole point is to provide these services for our community and get
our community exposed and at the same level as, like, any other big
name-brand companies." Connie, however, expressed goals of working in the film industry as well as with SFETT Pro: "For me, I would
really like to see some of us in the film industry, or some of us at a
higher level than just doing high school movies, I mean, independent
labels or however we can, as long as we can expose ourselves more to
different things."
Miguel confirmed that he would like to be a director:

Mostly because it's fun. For me, directing is fun, because I get to
show the world my point of view. It's like watching the movie
through my eyes. . . . I want to direct my movies, I want to edit
them, I want to score them, I want to produce, I want to do
everything. So people will read the credits they like "Oh, this
guy, he knows what he's doing! He's doing everything." I'm like,
damn right, I'm doing everything. Why? I want to do it. I just
want to show the world you don't just have to do one certain
thing. I'm not limited to anything. The only limitation there is
me limiting myself.

Torres himself expressed some affinity for making films, and
Marek appeared in one of the films at the festival. Torres says:

The kids know that I'm the creative type. I want to make
movies, and they're realizing, hey, you know what, if we continue to do this, as we get more and more people and you never
know, we could be making our own feature films. We've already
done our own film festival. You know, everybody says, hey can
we submit our films into your festival, and we're like, you guys
can make your own film festivals, too. I mean, we didn't follow
any kind of special recipe or anything. Plus, it's a festival, in
Spanish, it's a *festiva*. It's a celebration, as opposed to a contest.

Still, Rosa expresses slightly different goals. She is an education
major who hopes to come back to the community. Many kids, she
says, can't wait to get out of the San Fernando Valley, but she asks,
"Why not just stay here, make the best of it, work with our city? . . .
I think we're just really trying to just stay here and make this a bet-

ter community instead of going out somewhere to a nice community already and just kind of fit in. . . . This is where we came from. . . . Why not make the best of it?"

I kept waiting for someone to say something negative or disparaging of the project, but I could not find anyone who would. When I asked students if there were any drawbacks to any of this, all they could say was that their parents complain that they're never home. Of course, I couldn't help noticing all of the Apple Computer posters on the wall (with such famous people as Einstein and Ghandi above the Apple logo). Everyone made a point of saying, "It's not the technology." But I wonder what, then, were all of those representatives of Apple doing there the night of the film festival? A contingent even flew in from Apple New Zealand. As I write this chapter in September of 2003, Microsoft (Apple's competitor) has announced it will help design a new $46 million public high school in Philadelphia that will infuse technology into every phase of the school's life. Of course, there is money to be made with new literacies.

Still, even though the SFETT lab had Apple posters on its walls, the kids I met were not "techies," or shills for Apple equipment. If anything, they sounded more like throwbacks to Judy Garland and Mickey Rooney in *Babes on Broadway* (Berkeley, 1941). The kids of SFETT wanted to put on a show for their community, complete with selling T-shirts, refreshments, and website consulting to boot. But it wasn't just a show. If anything, my observations at SFETT brought me closer to witnessing the realization of the concept of "edutainment" than anything I'd ever seen before. Perhaps the emphasis that SFETT has ultimately placed on video production is because of the natural progression from stills to motion, reminiscent of Dewey's (1902/1990) suggestion that children, as they are learning, parallel the progression of primitive humans up to the present. Dewey had theorized that a child's progression of emergent literacy and thinking skills paralleled the development of human communication seen over centuries, from cave drawings up through printed speech. In this modern situation, students began with Photoshop and progressed to full motion video editing, sent to a DVD for projection on a big screen in front of 250 people and to a worldwide audience on the SFETT website (http://www.sfett.net).

I asked Torres what he thought of the fact that several of his students are apparently going on to careers in education. He admitted that "in this community, the number one profession they choose, the ones that go to college, is teaching, and the reason for that is that the only educated people they see are teachers. . . . . There's an emotional connection there." However, he also gives this program some credit: "I think that they saw that learning was fun. . . . . I mean, you could teach all your subjects this way. You can do all of the projects and really have that kind of ownership and then share it with people. . . . . I know that it can live on."

As the summer daylight faded on the mild evening and the lights strung on trees in the courtyard began to glow, Marco Torres directed the students to assemble in front of the screens. The work accomplished, the students filed down the stairs and formed a huddle with some kneeling and some standing as one of the students said a prayer. They soon broke the huddle and films began to be projected. Suddenly, I felt as if I were in a San Fernando version of the film *Cinema Paradiso* (Tornatore, 1989), as the light flickered on the faces of the community members, laughing and watching and enjoying the sights that were projected on the outdoor screens.

The festival contained films of all genres, styles, topics. For example, each year, Torres has challenged his students to make an animation related to a Christmas theme. So for each of the last few years, students have created another installment in the "Snowfight" saga in which a snowman gets in trouble when he engages in a snowball fight. There were also short documentaries on water conservation and the life of Caesar Chavez. Finally, there were commercials for local establishments that the students had produced.

There was a real community atmosphere to the event, and the people laughed as they recognized local people who were acting in some of the videos. It was a packed courtyard that balmy night, and it seemed as if everyone knew everyone else. At the intermission, I heard one older man approach another older man and say, laughingly, "I didn't know that you could act. Can I have your autograph?"

Chapter 5

NEW LITERACIES AND THE SCHOOL LIBRARIAN

Profile: Sandy Bernahl, Peacock Middle School
Itasca, Illinois

At Peacock Middle School, the school librarian, or media center director, has attempted to collaborate with her teacher teams to infuse new technologies into the everyday life of the school. Her principal and school district have supported her and the school with a new literacies environment that includes software, cameras, and several computers with enough gigabytes for video editing and other multimedia production. When Sandy Bernahl, Media Center Director of Peacock Middle School, first started corresponding to tell me about the work that she and her teachers were doing, I began to feel that this would be a good school to study. What emerged from the data was the important role to be played in new literacies instruction by the school librarian. Indeed, before my time at Peacock Middle School was out, I had met teachers of science, reading and language arts, social studies, and industrial technology, all of whom were encouraging their students to learn content via multiple forms of representations, and much of this activity was apparently due to the tireless efforts of Bernahl. Her mission is to help with the units the teachers are doing and to be an advocate for various technology pieces that might inform their pedagogy.

In this chapter, I will refer to Sandy Bernahl as a "school librarian" and to her media center as a "library." I want to be clear about what I am describing; the position of Media Director for some school districts would be quite different from the job Bernahl has—in some districts, such a position might include ordering media products for the entire district, for example, or it might even be a public relations job. It is significant, however, that Bernahl and her district see her job as being more of a Media Director—that is, working with all media, not only print-based media.

THE SETTING

Peacock Middle School, of School District 10, is located in the extremely well-groomed suburb of Chicago called Itasca, just southwest of O'Hare airport. Much of the impetus for an emphasis on technology at the school has come from Peacock's principal, Reinhard Nickisch, who explained that he was first intrigued with using new technologies as a way of motivating students. Nickisch remembered his visits to see television production and multimedia presentations at other schools:

> These kids were so motivated to accelerate and to achieve and to make a presentation that they could be proud of. That doesn't suggest that the traditional forms of communications are obsolete or . . . are not appropriate. This was a tool that motivated these students to achieve and provide them with a sense of accomplishment and success, an elevated status, even among peers. . . . We had kids at school here that had difficulties achieving, but yet were so literate with technology. We had kids that were getting the Ds and the Fs and were not part of the aggregate here at school, part of the mainstream, you know felt isolated, but when you really looked deeply into their lives, you saw them able to navigate through technology much quicker than the majority. And I thought, if we could establish a technology base that included what we have upstairs, that included the [television] studio among other multimedia opportunities, we could connect with a far broader scope of kids.

Sandy Bernahl traces her involvement with new literacies to her graduate work at Northern Illinois University; as part of that work, she did an internship with Betty LaLiberte, school librarian at York High School in Elmhurst, Illinois. The York High library had what was called a "creativity center"—a room that included video production equipment as well as multimedia production software loaded on computers. During this time, Bernahl was also influenced by visiting a library administered by Gail Bush at Des Plaines High School. This library also had a section containing production equipment. Bernahl was intrigued with the notion that a school library could be a place for production as well as consumption of resources.

Bernahl feels that in some cases "old-fashioned" school librarians have ceded their leadership in new literacies to other professional educators in schools, and she sees this as abdicating a crucial responsibility. When I asked why she thought this has happened, she answered, "A lot of [school librarians] . . . have failed to keep up with technology, and . . . they have given it up to other teachers." She remarked that, in many schools the video studio has become connected to the Business Education Department or is overseen by a technology director or a technology teacher. "I think it's the fault of the media specialist/librarian profession for not taking responsibility," said Bernahl. "And some of it may be political on the part of their district administrations, too." When I asked what she meant by this, she answered:

> I'm getting into a very touchy subject here. I think it's very important for a media director not just to be able to handle information in all kinds of formats; they need to be able to use it as a role model to their students and to the faculty. And if they can't use it, have ownership over it, and know it, they're going to find somebody else is going to take it over for them. You will find that in the national NETS standards (http://cnets.iste.org), I believe. There is an incredible overlap between what the media director is supposed to be doing and the technology consultant. I'm kind of disappointed to see that, but I realized that that's where the vacuum was, and some states have a completely different idea. In Massachusetts, [the librarian] will only handle the information part, and then they have a technologist come in and handle only the technology, so they have this big divide, so to speak, and I don't see the wholeness of the big picture coming in together under one person. I think you really need that.

Certainly, at Peacock Middle School, the concept of the school librarian who can help with production as well as consumption of media has been actively embraced by Bernahl and Nickisch. Over the last 5 years, Bernahl and Nickisch have transformed the school's library into a true resource center for new literacies, complete with a fully functioning television studio and multimedia production suite.

One of the goals for the school is to eventually have a student-produced news and public affairs program that is broadcast within the school and to the community. Bernahl has also been very involved with the teachers and their instructional planning, helping them, as she visited with each team once a week, to support entire units with technology applications. Nickisch said, "Sandy's primary responsibility is to be the resource leader, and 'resource' is such a broad umbrella."

LIBRARY IN ACTION

The library at Peacock Middle School has become the hub for new literacies in the school, with classes coming to the library not only to be researchers of media, but producers of media as well. Bernahl has worked with teams of teachers to help them use the new literacies no matter the content being taught. Over the last several years, she and the teachers have worked to develop a series of assignments at each grade level that build on the students' abilities to navigate the new literacies, especially focusing on video production. Bernahl has developed a video production scope and sequence statement that guides the types of assignments teachers give at each grade level (see Figure 5.1). What is interesting about her purposeful positioning of the library as a center for production and consumption of media is that the library becomes a part of the daily work of teachers of all disciplines in all three grade levels.

A Language Arts Class

During my visit, I observed a library that was filled with students reading and writing in various texts. Michael Poremba's seventh-grade reading and language arts students were busy in the television studio, preparing video versions of Homer's *Odyssey*. Small groups of students were each responsible for one of the episodes from the adventures of Ulysses. Each group was expected to write a summary of the episode they had been assigned, according to criteria for writing effective summaries that had been discussed by Poremba and the class. Once summaries were written, group members were to find still pictures and other resources on the internet and these images were to be incorporated into a newscast version of the episode to be taped in the library's video production studio.

I asked Poremba what he felt working in the studio added to his class, and he responded, "Students have to prepare; they know they're going to be filmed; they know they're going to be in the studio. They do seem to like it. . . . The good thing is it works with reading, writing, speaking. . . . So it really is 'the language arts' that way." Poremba also feels that another positive element to the assignment is that students work together in groups, with one person serving as the stage manager, one as the director, and so on. Another important facet of working in video for Poremba is that it emphasizes the concept of audience—each class will be seeing the videos of the *Odyssey* summaries from each of his other classes. They will be watching their classmates perform, rather than just turning in a written essay that would be seen only by the teacher. Poremba touched on the social nature of literacy when he commented that "very few people write in isolation."

A Music Class

One of the teachers at Peacock who has been deeply involved with utilizing multiple literacies has been music teacher Bryen Travis. He described what one class does in the media center:

> We use Finale Notepad, which is a software program that allows you to use formal notation, and we'll do something where the students work on a piano piece—let's say it's Beethoven's Ninth and they work on a two-handed part with the harmony. They notate it out on the computer, working on the melody first with the right hand, and they work on acoustic piano with the left-hand harmonies and print it out. The computer will play it out for them. It will also tell them if they have it correct or incorrect in conjunction with learning the piano, which is one big unit that the seventh graders do. They work on hand-to-paper initially and then the computer gives them feedback on how it sounds.

Travis added that the students would then turn the notation into an MP3 file, and the class will listen to each file together and grade them on a final rubric.

In the library, I observed Travis's students using the desktop video editing software to work on another project in which students create commercials that are set to music. Travis explained the project to me: "I view commercials as a primary, the dominant art form in our culture in conjunction with music and how music is applied to improve the commercials, give them more emotional impact, if you will." Students were taught the basics of shooting and editing over a period

FIGURE 5.1 Video Production Scope and Sequence Statement

Level One
Sixth Grade

The sixth-grade team has committed to using their common time to team-teaching video curriculum projects, which will be repeated every quarter. This will allow the entire sixth grade to cycle through the studio at least twice. . . . Curriculum areas include language arts puppet plays based on a literature unit, with scriptwriting, a new skill. Science classes start with basic research using print and Internet resources in the Media Center. We cover the Big 6 skills and how to do a bibliography first, then students create a report on a dinosaur and a large group poster for their prop in the studio. Students present their report in a studio taping, learning studio basics. At the end of the sixth-grade year, classes come in to give oral reports over various countries thereby reinforcing everything learned so far. In each grade level, the four stages of a video production will be covered: planning and scripting; rehearsals; taping; and editing. At this level, editing will be discussed as a whole-class project.

Level Two
Seventh Grade

Seventh grade is now adding a common time to their grade level and is in the planning stage of how they will use video curricular projects. Projects include: This Day in History; demonstrating geometric shapes on camera; student book talks; weather fore-casting; and video research on careers. Regarding editing, students may begin to use the basic tools on the Avid editing system. Clips and subclips are planned out and put in the timeline by students under supervision. Simple Avid transitions and titles are used. Picture-in-picture can be used. Projects may be rendered out to a zip drive, CD, or DVD.

Level Three
Eighth Grade

Eighth grade has several curriculum research projects that culminate in a studio taping. Science classes do a unit on a scientist, creating a bound book about the person with pictures and their findings. The element that the scientist discovered is animated in its electron configuration as well. The book, pictures, poster, or other props are used in their speech on this person in the studio. A World Cultures unit is done on a country with a news event of that country done in a news magazine format. General music classes create a commercial, and language arts classes provide a Media Literacy unit. Productions may utilize the Chroma Key and use of special effects on the Avid com-puter. Students in general music create music videos. Ongoing projects throughout the year will include taping concerts, special events, book talks, news show segments, live news shows, and sports. Students will have many opportunities to learn and hone their skills in many ways under the supervision of many teachers.

of 4 days. The assignment is to storyboard, shoot, and edit a commercial that contains eight scenes. "They have to shoot this, edit it out, plan the music to it, bring it down here, export it, and the rest of the class views it, and it's great," said Travis. Each person in a group of four rotates through four jobs, with the point of the project being that they can use the tools later in the quarter when they will be expected to create a Ken Burns–style video based on a great composer.

When I asked what Travis would say to critics who might say that his is a general music class where the kids should be learning about music and not video production, he answered:

> If they do a video project on Mozart or Chopin, I think they're going to learn more than if they did a written report and presented it to the class, or even if they did a PowerPoint. There's just something about the technology that's so interactive. [It] provides such visual stimulus that they really work to make a good product to share with the class. In some ways, I don't get the kids up to Impressionism and the twentieth century in any depth. . . . But I think it's more important to hit things more in depth than to cover everything all at once. I'd be willing to bet that these kids are going to remember these projects for years and years and years to come.

I wondered how much time overall Travis spent during his general music class covering video production skills. He responded that he spends just a few days working on such basics as principles of camera placement and types of shots. Students who want to go beyond this are welcome to spend extra time in the library being tutored by Bernahl and other teachers. "I'm trying to teach music and not the complete videography class," said Travis. "It's a compromise. These are the tools, but not the end-all. You're not trying to make the class what it's not. You're still teaching music; these are just the tools." Travis felt that there would never be a separate computer course taught at the school, but that new technologies would always be integrated through course content to serve the district's curriculum goals.

Ultimately, a grade is assigned to the project based on a rubric that Travis designed. The students must have eight scenes, plus a title screen, a credit screen, dissolves, a fade to black, a fade from black, and transitions. Travis listed some other qualities he is looking for in the finished product:

The titles—can you read them? Are they clear? Audio? Where
they put the music. Storyboards—are they approved, are they
complete? . . . Did they use the angles? Is the message concise
or is it confusing? Are there disjointed scenes? . . . Does it make
sense? Is it visually stimulating? . . . The edits—are they well
done? . . . When I say visually stimulating, we talk about how
did you use the camera shots and angles. Is the person at one
side of your view screen, or did they fill the view screen? Do
you know what's going on? Do you have the same level eye contact with the camera every time? Do you have it high? Do you
have it from an oblique angle? All these things make it more
stimulating when the children watch it, and I'll often find that a
group will tape something, put it in the computer and say,
"Wait, that wasn't what I had in mind. Can I go back and retape
that?" If they're not behind, I'll usually let them do one or two
scenes that way. But then they go and figure out how they could
improve it. . . . There's a lot of technical things that I grade on
this project, but this is a 5-day project. . . . There are some
groups that don't get done and then it's outside class time. If
they don't get done, they have to work on it after school. . . . I'm
pretty strict about having the project done, or else the kids'll
take forever to do it.

When I asked Travis if he felt guilty that he is taking time from
the music content to teach video production, he said that he doesn't
feel guilty, that he feels he is meeting the board's goals for his general music class; he sees the technology as tools that help students
retain content. He added:

And you know what? The principal bought it. I mean, he saw
it at another school. He liked it; they allocated that much
money and I'm always willing to try new things. And I might
not be doing this forever. I mean, I've changed my curriculum
year in and year out. I work around the goals and that's what
I'm supposed to do as a teacher. You know, I could teach the
same thing every year, but I don't need a pile of brown lesson
plans and a filing cabinet from 20 years. Add a little variety to
it. For myself too.

A Science Class

Nancy Krefetz, an eighth-grade science teacher, also credited
Principal Nickisch and Librarian Bernahl with motivating her to uti-

lize new literacies. "Our principal is very much, you know, 'Technology is the future. So, you know, learn about it, learn about it.' So I just figured, well, I have to make the boss happy, so I will learn and it's been a good experience." Krefetz remembered being terrified of computers, terrified that she would press a button that would cause "the world to end." Slowly but surely, Bernahl kept bringing up software programs that would serve the science curriculum.

In one of Krefetz's assignments, designed with the help of Bernahl, students were to draw out an electron configuration, create an animated three-dimensional simulation of the element in Crystal 3D, render the animation as an AVI file, and insert it into a PowerPoint slide that summarizes the basic facts about the element. Saving the animation as an AVI file allows the viewer to click on an icon and see the electrons moving. For the first step in the assignment, Krefetz asked students to research how atoms affected such modern technologies as CAT scans and carbon dating. Once students had researched the answer, they put their answers into Director, which she described as "a more advanced version of PowerPoint." The next step of the assignment was that students used a program called Crystal 3D to arrange their atom according to protons and neutrons in their orbits. "This takes a little doing at first," said Krefetz, "because they have to make a key and decide how many, what color neutrons would equal on two electrons, ten electrons. So they have to vision in their mind how they're going to set up their atom."

Krefetz said that the students resisted Director at first, wanting to keep using PowerPoint, but she challenged them to use this new technology:

> I told them that, you know, they're older now, they have to start learning new things. Even if they only use it once. So one thing I hope they learn is they have to learn about change; they can't keep status quo. [They also have] to work in groups, I think, on a more advanced level. They have to decide the music; they have to decide what is going to be placed on each page format. So it's a deeper level, I think.

Indeed, Krefetz pointed to working in groups as being one of the most salient outcomes of this kind of teaching.

> It took a lot of cooperation, and it was very very difficult for them. Very difficult. . . . But I find, you know, especially at this age, they have to learn to work together; they have to learn to make decisions; and so it's not only, "What is an atom made

of?" It's also your character. . . I just think it's overall, you
know, what it does for the human being—they learn technology;
they learn to think critically; they have to cooperate; they have
to learn to solve their own problems.

During the 2003–04 school year, Krefetz developed a new unit
called Change, Technology, and Society that included an Invention
Convention. Students videotaped interviews with patent lawyers
who came to the school to evaluate student inventions. Portions of
these videos can be viewed on the school's website: http://itas-
ca.k12.il.us/peacock/

WHAT THE STUDENTS SAY

When I was in the library, students were working on their video
projects for Bryen Travis's eighth-grade general music class. The
groups were each huddled around a computer terminal, loudly discussing the cuts they wanted to make. I asked Linda what her group's
project was about. "A person who's getting ignored and doesn't have
a lot of friends or anything, and basically she bumps into me and we
push her around and pretend that she's not there," she answered.
Kathy joined in: "She doesn't exist. And so, at the end, we're doing
transitions about how she fades into us, like she's not even there.
She's walking down the steps because she's lower." Kathy explained
further: "And then we have to put it on the computers. We have to
write a storyline that has who's the director, the editor, and then we
put it all together with the song 'Complicated' by Avril Lavigne. [Mr.
Travis] picks the song. Everyone's done the same song." Linda
explained, "We all had to do [each] job at least one time."

When I asked why they think this kind of assignment is worth
doing, Linda answered, "They want us to learn it so that when we go
to the high school, we'll know what to do. . . . We can have more
experience in editing, so later on in life if we want to do this [we
can]." I pointed out that they might not all want to become video edi-
tors. Amy answered, "It's still a great experience. I mean, when
you're like . . . Say, you know, you become a father, so, you know,
you're at the dance recital for your daughter and you're filming. It's
really great to know how to use electronics, because they're becoming more popular and everything's becoming, basically, all about
technology." Linda continued: "Because technology is going way far-
ther in today's future and stuff so technology with TVs and comput-

ers will go . . . who knows maybe like 15 years . . .there's going to be way more stuff."

When I asked if it has changed the way they watch television, several of the students responded that they have more appreciation for all of the work that an editor has to go through to make each cut. Linda talked about the challenges they had faced: "Yeah. . . . We had trouble . . .we had trouble with some of the scenes because they weren't clicking as right into those scenes, so we were going to, like, reshoot it, but then we thought that we should just cut some of it out."

I asked if they had any disagreements in their group. "Well, yeah," said Linda. "We were thinking of reshooting the scene, but then we thought that it would take too long to reshoot the scene, so we just, like, did some transitions and special effects, and we got it to work."

When I talked to some of the students who had done the animated models of the atom, they all spoke about how much fun that project was. "You're working with your friends," one boy said. Also, several of the students felt they had learned the content better than if they had been studying the atom out of a textbook. Angela said, "I find that monkeying around with text helps you learn it, because you're seeing it constantly." Martin agreed: "Because you would accidentally delete your stuff. You'd have to retype it, [and so] you'd learn it. You'd have to get your presentation done, so you'd memorize it."

Often students would refer to the career benefits they felt they were gaining by working in new literacies. Rob thought their experiences would be helpful:

> It would especially help if one day you were planning to work as a scientist or computer engineer or something, because you're getting early experience that most kids don't get at this age level of how to work with different types of electronics. We've got a lot of programs here at school, especially like Director. . . . That's a program that's used in professional level projects for many professions, so we're getting a lot of experience that a lot of kids don't have. It's really becoming important in today's society.

When I asked Rob about the video project he did in the general music class and whether he thought this project really taught him much about music, he answered in terms of technology benefits:

> Well, you know, composers of music today aren't anything like composers in the past who had to write down all the notes. We

have a lot of really advanced equipment these days. There's programs like, uh, I think it's called Notepad. It will draw the notes up for you, and by doing videography, and stuff like that and working with those types of programs, you get the knowledge of how to work a computer, and that can come in handy if you ever decide to compose a piece of music one day.

Linda added, "Well, even if you don't become something like that, having to do with music and technology, it's still great experience. It's always great to do some of this stuff. It's a lot of fun. I had a lot of fun doing it."

I asked what is so much fun about these kinds of projects. Amy, referring to the electron project, answered, "Mostly getting to the point of seeing your project come to life. I mean, at the end, you get to click a button and then it'll just rotate, it'll rotate all the little electrons." Rob was amazed by seeing how many electrons there are in one element. "It's just amazing," he said. "You get to see up close, really. After you put it all together, you see what is created. It's really amazing." Amy agreed: "It's a visual of how complex an atom is, and it's awesome to see it." "Rather than just a page in a book," added Rob. When I asked them why they think this kind of project helps them learn, Rob answered:

> Well, some students learn better reading, . . . and some learn visually. Some need to have a teacher sit there and explain to them or draw them a picture. And instead of having the teacher draw them a picture, they're doing it themselves. They actually created it; it's probably helping them better understand.

When I ask Amy what her element was, she can't name it, but she says that she never got to finish her project. Rob's element was uranium. I ask him if he remembers the characteristics of uranium. He responded,

> I remember I had to draw up each little electron. It has 98 or 99 electrons in the shell, and I had to make . . . it was so many electrons, that I couldn't just make one electron each, 'cause it would just be a solid color if I did that, 'cause it would just fill up the entire screen. So I remember that I had to assign a certain amount of electrons to different colors of the spheres, so it took a while. It would have taken a lot longer if I had done just one electron each time.

The students admitted that they miss the technology when they go to other classrooms where it is not used. Rob spoke for the group:

I don't think anybody wants to sit there. They want to get into it. They want to be involved. . . . Everybody can do something. Even people, you know, maybe in the mentally challenged class. They were even there in my group and they can do anything too. It's just something for everyone.

ROLE OF LIBRARIAN

When I talked to teachers at Peacock, time and again, they brought up the efforts of Sandy Bernahl, the school's librarian. Bernahl was described as "a risk-taker," "very helpful," and "an expert in the building." She was also praised for always letting teachers and students take ownership over projects. Teachers also mentioned her unique role in the school's organization system in that she is not an administrator and can't "force" any teacher to change his or her pedagogy. "Sandy is so good at helping teachers incorporate this stuff into their classes, it's not intimidating," said Bryen Travis. "She goes around to team meetings," said Nancy Krefetz. "She'll give us information on new websites, websites that would help us with technology, websites that will help us with lessons. She'll also, like I said, she'll get new programs in that she might be interested in herself, and she'll say, 'Oh, this would be a good one for science.'"

Bernahl summed up her philosophy about the role of the librarian in the school:

I realized . . . that my library was no longer going to be an old-fashioned one where you just find the information. But it also [would] include producing and communicating. So that meant a big switch, I guess you would say, in the direction of where libraries were going. Then ISLMA—The Illinois School Library and Media Association—came out with their guideline and it is called *Linking for Learning,* and in the back it talks about "essential components to consider," and these are areas an old-fashioned library has not gotten into, but this was right down my alley. Just listen to this: "You have the traditional things of print, periodicals, electronic, CD-Roms, video networks, internet, intranet, fax, emerging technologies—e-books, wireless, DVD, assistive technologies. In your service area, you would include reference: internet, video, multimedia, interactive media, media production, and communication, recreation, performance storytelling, and distance learning." Everything I wanted to do! So it's been approved by the state of Illinois. Now what I find very interesting is that a lot of libraries haven't even thought about getting into this yet.

Bernahl felt that a key reason that some media specialists haven't taken the lead they need to take regarding new literacies was their own fear of the technology. "You have to know how to edit yourself before you can teach someone else how to edit," she said. "Information comes in all kinds of formats. It's not limited to print. . . . If it contains information, then it should be part of the media specialist's domain."

When I asked her where she would like to go from here, she answered,

I want to get into interactive media more. I need to take a workshop myself on DirectorMX, 'cause that can be interactive—put it on the web and you can have interactive choices, so I would like to do some instructing modules. . . . I think the sky's the limit. I foresee holographic software coming in. . . . I would love to see robotics come in here into the multimedia some kind of way. I think that would be exciting. I'm not sure how that would happen, but I'm certainly open to ideas. So I don't think there's any limit to multimedia.

POSTSCRIPT

In December, 2003, Sandy wrote me with some updates:

We have started out with Mr. Travis's sixth-grade advisory group doing daily live announcement video broadcasts. They are going very well. These sixth graders had to learn how to use many complex machines and skills to produce a live show. This advisory group will train Nancy Krefetz's advisory next who will take over in January. Each of us on the Newscast Committee will have our advisory group do live newscasts for several weeks until school is out in June. . . .

My role has become much more of a collaborator-teammate, with these teachers taking the leadership role. The Media

Center has become more of a support to these teachers instead of my trying to initiate things as happened when we first started several years ago. I am grateful to see the leadership roles take off in exciting ways. I foresee they will initiate exciting new things. This is a faculty you might want to revisit somewhere down the road.

I had not originally set out to profile a school librarian as part of this study, but spending time with Bernahl helped me see the crucial role a school librarian can play in building up critical mass for using new literacies. Bernahl saw herself as part of the instructional teams within the school, spending as much time out of the library meeting with teachers during their team meetings as she did in the library. She demonstrated how the school librarian can be a force for breaking down walls of disciplines and for (literally) creating space for production of media in a school library.

It was noticeable that during the time that I spent at Peacock and in follow-up emails and phone communication, I never heard Bernahl or any of the teachers speak at the critical analysis level of working in new literacies as advocated by Freebody and Luke (1990) and the New London Group (1996). It was clear that Bernahl and the teachers were most intent on teaching the students to implement new literacies at the functional-operational level, training students to use new software and hardware almost as fast as they would appear on the market. The focus for using the tools was squarely on using them to enhance the teaching of the curriculum content and to prepare students for high school and college and career tasks. During the brief time I visited the school, I did not hear discussion, for example, of how forms familiar to middle schoolers, such as music videos or fan fiction websites position teenagers in society. Perhaps in no small way, however, the educators at Peacock Middle School were empowering these middle school students by teaching them how to use the most current tools so that they were enabled at least to take part in the current discourse. Certainly students expressed relief that their librarian and their teachers were creating a space for multimedia production in the library.

Chapter 6

NEW LITERACIES AND AT-RISK STUDENTS

Profile: Lee Rother
Lake of Two Mountains High School
Deux Montagnes, Quebec

Two boys begin singing a rap song in French; they are hanging out of windows of a school bus about to depart at the end of the school day. They assure me that when I come back tomorrow they will be able to perform a rap song in English. "I didn't even know that there was French rap." "OK, sir, you didn't know that?" they say. "We'll see you tomorrow, sir." It is a custom here to refer to male teachers as "Sir" and female teachers as "Miss." I was not used to being addressed as "Sir" by my own students in Ohio.

And I was certainly not used to the amazing level of bilingualism I was encountering here in Montreal, where people of all ages are able to switch between languages without effort and sometimes with hardly a trace of accent. I was visiting Deux Montagnes, a suburb of Montreal, to observe Lee Rother, a teacher who has broken out of the rigid codes of a print-dominated pedagogy, and who has done this in an alternative setting—an "at-risk" classroom for students who have, at the age of 16, reached "the end of the line." In fact, the at-risk nature of his students was what had pushed Rother into reconceptualizing his English classroom. I had seen new literacies in college preparatory environments. How would new literacies play out in an "alternative" school?

I had met Rother through an electronic mailing list (media-l@nmsu.edu). Rother (2000, 2002) had studied his own practice and determined that his students "read and write media texts with considerable sophistication," "were able to identify ideologies in a text and relate them to their own experiences," and "were more willing to undertake the kind of school writing they are expected to do, using media texts as a source for their writing" (2002, p. 16). When he invited me to see his classroom, I eagerly accepted.

THE SETTING AND THE PROGRAM

Lake of Two Mountains (LTM) High School in Deux Montagnes is a school of 550 seventh- through eleventh-grade students outside of Montreal. Rother teaches in what's known as a "16 plus" program that is housed at LTM. This is an alternative cooperative education (ACE) program for students aged 16 to 18, who might have dropped out without such a program. In the United States, these kinds of programs are often referred to as "work-study" programs, although Rother's program has some major differences from those in the United States.

The students in Rother's class have been referred from guidance counselors and other feeder schools within the school district (the Sir Wilfrid-Laurier School Board). This school district includes students who live in the communities surrounding Montreal: Deux Montagnes, St. Eustache, Oka, Rosemere, and others. Oka is an Indian reserve. Without Rother's "16 Plus" program, the students would have nowhere to go. These are students who have not been successful within traditional educational settings. But, as Rother points out, "What they are really at risk from is the educational system itself!"

One of the main differences I saw between Rother's program and "work-study" programs in the United States is that Rother's students are perhaps even more marginalized than students in work-study programs. His students are no longer on course to obtain a high school diploma (which in Canada occurs after grade 11). Most work-study students in the United States, if they stay in school, will receive a high school diploma when they graduate. Students come to Rother having finished (or not finished) a variety of levels of English and math. After spending 2 years with Rother and his coteacher in the ACE program, students will receive only a "certificate in life skills and work skills" from the Ministry of Education. The students do not receive a "high school certificate," but they do obtain credits in the "core subjects" toward receiving that high school certificate. While in the program, students participate in on-the-job training in local business and industry as well as work in various in-school business-es. Rother explained: "Part of each semester, students are based in school where they work in teams on group projects developing their English, French, and math skills. Part of each semester, students con-tinue their learning on the job. Each student has a training plan devel-oped to meet his or her interests and career goals." After finishing the ACE program, students may enter further education or vocational training.

New Literacies

The first morning that I observed Rother's class, I entered as stu-dents were watching a television monitor intently and counting the number of cuts in the famous shower sequence in Hitchcock's *Psycho* (Hitchcock, 1960). "52!" one would shout. "No, 55!" "Sir, please start it again." Each student had a storyboard open on his or her desk with each individual shot of the shower sequence numbered. This famous sequence, in which the character played by Janet Leigh is brutally attacked in a shower, is made up of a number of different individual camera shots, meticulously assembled by Hitchcock and his editor. As each shot would come on the screen, the students would say the shot number out loud. Later in the morning, the whole class chanted in unison the shot numbers as they examined a story-board for the crop duster sequence in *North by Northwest* (Hitchcock, 1959), watching the scene with the sound turned off. The students were learning how to "read" the text of a Hitchcock film and they seemed very accomplished as they were able to quickly chant the shot numbers without missing one, even during this fast-paced scene.

I noticed that three students were in an adjoining room working at computers. Two students were working together on a Flash ani-mation project, and the remaining student was in another corner by himself editing a video. The solitary student's assignment was to edit together some raw video footage from a family wedding that Rother brought to school. The student was expected to weave the raw footage together into a coherent story. As I watched over his shoul-der, his first title card read: "Once upon a time, there was a beautiful maiden." I asked Rother why these students weren't with the rest of the class, and he answered that he felt these three students were bet-ter off working on these alternative projects. It didn't seem to bother him or the other students that these students were off working on their own projects.

In October 2002, when I visited Rother's class, there were 44 students in the program, mostly white males, ranging from age 15–19. Rother shared these students during the day with another teacher who mainly taught math. Rother had most of the students during Periods 1 through 3 when he taught them English. During Periods 4 through 6 he taught World of Work, which Rother also infused with new literacies. "Depending on what we're doing, sometimes we'll keep the kids all together and sometimes we'll split them to go to the labs, or sometimes we'll do work in class," Rother said. Rother explained that the students don't have social studies or science during the 2 years they are with him. "See, the kids don't graduate from high school [at the end of this program]," he explained. "We don't do all the subjects leading to graduation. Frankly, we don't have the time, and the other thing, too, is most of the kids come with so few credits, in 2 years there's just no way they're going to get the credits with us."

When I asked Rother what they'd be working on during my visit, he answered that he was right in the midst of a unit that compares and contrasts different print and nonprint versions of the Snow White story, focusing on visual languages, storyboarding, connotation, denotation, and embedded advertising. On one of the mornings I observed, Rother was in a large-group setting, and was leading the students through an exercise in which they compared and contrasted Disney's *Snow White and the Seven Dwarfs* (Hand, 1937) with a newer film, Michael Cohn's *Snow White: Tale of Terror* (Cohn, 1997). First, Rother showed approximately 10 minutes from each film, instructing students to "read" these clips. In fact, the entire morning, students used the term *read* instead of *view* or *watch* when they referred to seeing a film clip. Students were expected to answer questions about features such as color, music, genre, point of view, plot, and characters; for example: "How is color used to create mood?" "Is what happens in the first 15 minutes the same, different?" "What is the setting (time and place)? How do we know this?" and "Are there any characters who exist in one but not the other?" Later, students will read printed versions of the Snow White story from various countries.

But Rother and the students don't stop at the functional-operational level (New London Group, 1996; Freebody & Luke, 1990) of reading texts. When reading a text such as the film *The Siege* (Zwick, 1998), for example, Rother not only asked questions related to genre,

FIGURE 6.1 Questions for Comparing and Contrasting Film Versions of Snow White

---

Disney's *Snow White and the Seven Dwarfs* and Michael Cohn's *Snow White: Tale of Terror*

1. (a) How is color used to create mood? Explain.
   (b) How are music and sound effects used?
   (c) Is what happens in the first 15 minutes the same, different? Explain.
   (d) What kind of visual language (cuts, transitions, dissolves) are used to move from one scene to another?
   (e) What genre is the Disney version? What conventions (ingredients) tell us this?
   (f) What genre is the Cohn version? What conventions (ingredients) tell us this?
   (g) What is the setting (time and place)? How do we know this?

2. (a) How is the story told? From whose point of view? Voice over? If so, is the voice one of the characters or an unknown narrator?
   (b) How is the story told through the action itself?
   (c) Do any of the characters talk directly into the camera or do the actors pretend the camera is not there?
   (d) Where are you as the audience?
   (e) Are there any shifts in locations in either version? If so, what are they?

3. (a) Explain how the characters listed below are similar and different.
   (b) Match the characters in *Tale of Terror* with the characters in Disney's version.
   (c) Are there any characters who exist in one but not the other?
   Characters: Snow White, Lillian, Stepmother, Lady Claudia, Witch, Father, Stepmother's brother Gustaf, Huntsman, Thieves, Seven dwarves, Peter, Prince Charming

4. How is the plot in *Tale of Terror* the same and different from the Disney version?

5. (a) Create a sociogram in which you use a different color line to indicate the relationship between the different characters. For example, you could use a red line to indicate love between Lord Hoffman and Lillian. Make a legend for each relationship.
   (b) Did some of the relationships change over the course of the narrative? If so, make a second sociogram to indicate the changes in the relationships.

---

such as "Was there any use of color that stood out to you?" and "How did the mood of the music add to the movie?", he also asked questions that made connections to today, such as "Considering the attacks on September 11, do you think *The Siege* would have been released today?" and "In *The Siege*, Denzel Washington's FBI partner, played by Tony Shalhoub, is of Arab extraction: What does Shalhoub's role say about the image of Arab Americans?" (See Figure 6.2).

Is This English?

Why does Rother do these kinds of activities in an alternative school during a class that's titled "English?" When I asked Rother how he got started in all of this, he told a story that happened at the beginning of his teaching career, in 1977:

> I was an art major. When I graduated, it was one of the worst years for new teachers, and somebody said, why don't you take some special ed? I didn't even know what special ed was at the time. It was the best thing that ever happened to me as far as I'm concerned, because as you know, I teach the kids not the subjects. . . . So that's how I got into it. I started in 1977 and finished the Master's in 1986 . . . but what got to me was the Master's had nothing to do with media and technology. I was looking at self-concept and special ed kids. I finagled a portable TV studio—black and white, two cameras and a switcher, and the kids were doing this Bandura kind of thing where the kids would reenact an episode based on their family or peers and then redo that, how they would have liked to see it go, OK? Very dangerous and naive! But this one kid named Ron, 17 or 18, reading at a Grade 4 level, and he was the switcher, and he came back to school one day after being the switcher for maybe a week, he came to me and said, "I can't watch TV anymore." And I thought maybe he got in trouble or something at home, and he said, "No, no, it just doesn't make any sense." And I didn't know what he was talking about. So he went on to describe to me [that] he was watching this program, and he saw this woman was crying or something in it, and they had a medium shot or whatever and I asked him, what should they have had, and he said, "A close-up." And he went into this whole thing, and I didn't care if he was right or wrong. But this kid was "reading" it and he was making this whole language out of it, and I remember getting all excited and talking with the other kids and sure enough, they were saying the same things, and I haven't been able to let go of that whole thing since.

Rother pointed with some disdain at the two binders of objectives that he was supposed to teach:

The MEQ [Ministry of Education of Quebec] developers. . . . When I looked at the huge two binders of the objectives; it was a guide that was step-by-step how to teach, which I can't do. OK? I just can't do that. It was again 99 percent print. I mean one of the things I kept thinking was, these are kids, and to take them [adolescents] . . . to the world of work because they haven't been successful—seems a quantum leap and scary, and I've been told that by some of the kids. I mean, they're scared— 16, 17 even—and they're scared! . . . Well, part of the 16 plus program is to look at economics and family. What text are they familiar with, comfortable with? The media. . . . If they're famil- iar with that, again . . . they were talking about this stuff so nat- urally, and everything was there in terms of language arts, but they didn't know what they were saying in terms of conven- tions. They didn't know the word *conventions.* They didn't know what *plot* meant, but they were talking about it. So it just seems very natural.

Rother also credited pioneers in the field of media literacy for the revolution in his teaching. He cited attending the First Canadian International Media Literacy Conference as an important influence. He also cited the work of Eddie Dick (1991) of Scotland and Len Masterman (1986) of England. But Rother added, "I love TV!" You can tell this by how his room is decorated—the room is covered with movie posters and other media visual references. In fact, his huge *Star Wars* poster that hangs in his window is clearly visible from the street.

After his early years of seeing students learn literary conventions via nonprint media, Rother has continued to unite his own love for media and his motivation to help at-risk students into a variety of new literacies assignments and assessments. "Often when the kids come to my program, for all intents and purposes, they are mute," Rother stated. "In the sense that they've learned to shut up. Keep your mouth shut, and the teacher won't know that you don't know the answers. I want to get them talking. I'm an instigator. [I want them] yelling at each other in an organized way."

He used his current lesson, focusing on different versions of *Snow White,* as an example to illustrate his point:

Right now we're looking at texts, genres, conventions, and visual language. Today, they read *Snow White: Tale of Terror*. . . . That's live action with Sigourney Weaver and Sam Neill. . . . It's a psycho-thriller. It's a great movie, and the kids eat it up. I've tried this before with other groups. So they're reading that today in class, and they're also going to be looking at the first 15 minutes at least of the Disney version, and I've got a whole thing where they've got to look at the relationships and the visual language and the contrast and all that kind of stuff, but I'm trying to show them how these are different texts—basically the same story, but . . . different conventions are used, how lighting was used in this one, and so on, color. [See Figure 6.1.] That, to me, is visual language. The second part of this whole thing, though, is we have different versions of the written text of Snow White. One is the original Grimm, shortened. Another is from Italy, Germany, and I even have the "politically correct" Snow White (Garner, 1995). So they're going to take those and look at how language is used, how suspense is created using words. But that's not just deconstructing it. One of the things we're looking at in *Tale of Terror* is the relationships among the women in Snow White and the stepmother. But to me that's not a media thing; it's not just looking at gender. It's language, it's literary, it's dramatic, it's cinematic. I don't go by the terms in that sense. I want these kids reading and writing.

In addition to learning to read and write in multiple forms of texts, there is another layer to Rother's program: Students operate the media center for the entire district, which includes 36 schools. In 1994 the school board was forced to close the district's audiovisual and media center. Now, Rother's students, in addition to studying the film grammar of Hitchcock, also participate in video production for the schools as well as for outside clients and offer services such as graphic work and laminating, as well as cataloging and distribution of educational videos owned by the district.

When I asked Rother how he grades all of this, he responded that he is not a fan of rubrics, because he finds them limiting in that they sometimes narrow what students end up producing. He generally starts with a basic evaluation outline, which then is adapted to individual students. "In some instances," he said, "I actually have the students work with me on the evaluation tool. . . . I will consult with students as to how parts of a project should be weighted, for which they provide a rationale, as well as due dates. Of course, I have the final word."

FIGURE 6.2 Questions for *The Siege*

CLASS DISCUSSION

Literary/close-reading

- Who are the characters in the movie?
- What is the setting? (time and place)
- What is the plot?
- What is the mood of the movie?
- Did all, some or none of the events seem true? Did any sequence(s) not seem believable?
- From whose point of view was the story told? Is it told from anybody's point of view in particular (subjective) or nobody in particular (objective)?
- Who do you think is the target audience? What audience rating would you give this movie? Why?
- What is the theme of the movie? What were the makers of this film trying to tell us? (the message)
- How do you think the movie might be different from the book?
- Was there anything that you did not understand about the movie?

Dramatic genre: the look of the movie

- What did you like the best? What did you dislike the most?
- Who was your favorite actor and why? Who was your least favorite actor and why?
- Why do you think the actors were chosen for their parts?
- Select a character in the movie and explain why they took a specific action. What motivated them to do it? Do you feel they were right to do what they did?

Cinematic/technical aspects of the movie

- What images stand out in your mind? What sounds or words stand out?
- Was there any use of color which stood out to you? Why? What mood did the color create?
- Describe the type of music used. Was it original music? How did it add to the mood of the movie? Would you have used the same or different music? If different, what would you have used and why?
- How important is the setting? Could the events have occurred in another time or place? If yes, when and where? If not, why not?
- Was there anything special about the costumes or the way people were dressed? Did their dress, makeup, suit their role?
- What other movies are similar to this one? Explain how.

FIGURE 6.2 (continued)

PUTTING IT ALL TOGETHER; WRITTEN RESPONSES

- Choose a sequence or scene from the movie that you think is important and answer the following questions:
- Describe the sequence or scene; what happens?
- Why is this sequence or scene important to the plot?
- Are there any important or special camera angles, camera shots, camera movements, lighting, dialogue, sounds, music?
- What does the sequence or scene tell you about the character(s) in the movie?
- What is the mood of the sequence or scene and how is this created?

MAKING CONNECTIONS TO TODAY

- What did you learn in The Siege about how we react to terror, minority groups, group blame, revenge, anger?
- In what ways might we be able to connect the events and issues in The Siege to events that have occurred (are occurring) in society today, as a result of the September 11 attacks?
- Considering the attacks of September 11, do you think The Siege would have have been released today? If so, after how long a period? Would it attract more or less viewers if it was released today?
- If The Siege were released today, what do you think would be the reaction of people in the theatre watching it, of people in general?
- Imagine shooting for The Siege is in its genesis, and you are the producer; in light of the attacks, do you proceed or halt production and take your losses?
- What, if anything, might be the effect of the attacks on current and future media releases?
- In The Siege, Denzel Washington's FBI partner, played by Tony Shalhoub, is of Arab extraction: What does Shalhoub's role say about the image of Arab Americans?
- What personal, ideological, and legal conflicts confront the FBI agent?
- In The Siege, the FBI agent's son is interned. The FBI agent is furious at hearing that his son has been taken away. Pretend you are the agent, what are you thinking? Imagine you are the mother, what are you thinking? Imagine you are the son/daughter; write a diary entry describing your feelings as you are in the arena holding area. Write a dialogue between you and the FBI's son, just before he is taken away to the arena.

WHAT THE STUDENTS SAY

Several students in Rother's class talked about the experience of engaging with new textual worlds on a more sophisticated level. Steve described how he "reads" a movie:

Basically, it's taking down mental notes on everything that does happen in a movie—foreshadowing, for instance, like small things, like why things happen in a movie, and for what reason exactly—the background, the lighting, the mood, the settings. There's a lot of things that take place. . . . You just look at the movie differently. You realize it more.

Steve went on to analyze Disney's *Snow White and the Seven Dwarfs* (Hand, 1937):

It's a classic, I'd say. . . . The cartoon is so old fashioned that every page was drawn by hand. And you can tell the backgrounds are oil-pastel painted, basically. I find it's a lot better than today's 1-D, like, plain, color cartoons and stuff. . . . They took many years to put their time into it, with the hand drawing, one-by-one, every single page. They took a lot of time coloring each picture also. They had a lot of shading. Let's say, if someone had rosy cheeks, they would really show that it was rosy cheeks, pale skin, black hair. It really shimmered in the sun.

As I mentioned, I witnessed the students analyzing both the famous shower scene from *Psycho* and the crop duster scene from *North by Northwest.* Rother took some time to point out that there are some insert shots of Cary Grant during the crop duster scene where he is obviously in a studio and not on location. The next day, after this discussion, Steve brought in a skateboarding movie he owned for the class to analyze. Rother set aside what he had planned for a few minutes. Steve talked about how this is a movie he watched every day, primarily to study skateboarding moves, yet he pointed out that now he is "concentrating" more: "I don't just watch it and veg out. I'm concentrating on what I'm seeing and what I'm doing at the moment." Steve's comment signifies a step forward in being a critical reader-viewer of texts. Steve also saw a transfer of his skills at reading of film and video to his reading of print text skills. "When you read a book," he said, "you basically see it as if you are watching a movie, but you're reading. We learned to read a movie, so now, when you read a book, it's like, basically reading the movie." He admitted that he still doesn't read that often (if at all) for pleasure, but, he said,

> I read faster. I remember what I'm reading after it's done. Last year, I would pick up a book and just read fast. Like I've always had a fast reading level, but when I put the book down, I wouldn't remember what I just read—character names, the plot, the story, or the ending or anything, but now, like, the book I've just read, I feel as if I just finished watching a movie. I can go up to people—"Remember the part when that happened in?" It's improved my reading a lot. And I'm proud of it, because I enjoy reading a lot more now. Before it was just something boring thing that you dreaded to do and try to avoid. Now, well it's not that I do it more often or anything, but when the time comes, I'm not going to complain about it in any way.

I watched the students listen intently to Steve as he went through the skateboarding video, and they cheered at some of the exciting moves the skateboarder made. In interviews throughout my visit, students brought up the spirit of collaboration that they have experienced in this classroom. Sean said,

> I don't dread coming to school in the morning as I did in my previous school. . . . I even find out staying at home is boring. Back in my old school, I think I was in school, I think like 50 days out of the whole school year. I had no intention of waking up and going to school. I thought staying at home was funner. Now, I was sick one day and it was boring at home. And I had everything I could possibly do like TV, computer, Nintendo. It's just boring. It's not the same as it would be in school. In school, you have more interaction with the students and the teachers.

Working on the classroom business has also brought students into contact with the outside world. As Robert explained,

> Well, you learn to get along with everybody, since you met different people you've never seen before. You get along with them. You get to learn just about different things. I had to go to

the Jewish community and film these plays that were going on and help out in special aid to film their things that were going on. I learned a lot of different things.

Students also talked about their own personal growth. Steve said,

Yeah, well, it's excellent! I find I've grown up maturely, wise. I don't even know if that's a word—maturely. I have grown up tremendously since I've started here. Like 2 years ago I was really just like a spoiled brat, well not spoiled, but I was a real brat, you know, I'd pick on people, not listening to teachers, do whatever I wanted. Thought I was king of the world, but really, I was just like nothing. And I didn't listen to what anyone had to say, basically.

Students spoke fondly of Rother. Steve stated, "I don't know, he's like a father to me, basically. But he's like a big giant kid also, so he's like a brother, a kid, I don't know. Mr. Rother's a big kid; that's what I say." Indeed, students sometimes petition to stay a third year in the program, and Rother reported that students from the mainstream (not at-risk) school population ask to get into his program. "It's just that this works," he said.

It's not just the media and the technology. It's the whole community thing, as corny as that sounds, works. These kids, they want this. They have their own union. You know, they made their own union, so we have to negotiate. Every year, we initiate that, and try to get them to do that. You know what they call themselves this year? Every year, they can change it because a new executive comes in. They decided to call themselves "spACE Cadets." You know what, it's great. That's another thing, too—these kids take ownership of this program. They really, really do. I mean, it's so ironic, we've had kids from mainstream come to us and ask us to come into the program. People say, "How do you know you've been successful?" To me, never mind anything else, when a kid comes to us from the mainstream and says, "Can I come into your program?" To me that's a sign.

POSTSCRIPT

In February 2004, Rother took a new position with his school district. He will be Secondary English Language Arts/Media Education Consultant. In an email message, Rother wrote,

This includes such tasks as providing guidance and/or advice in implementing the curriculum. It is a huge challenge, as Quebec is in the genesis of implementing the massive Quebec Education Program (QEP) [reform] into the high schools next year, starting with Cycle One, which is Grades 7 and 8. The QEP is already in the elementary system, more or less. As expected, getting it into the high schools is going to take up much of my time. I am pushing the Media Lit stuff, as it is also mandated in the QEP, and most do not have a real concrete idea what that implies.

As for Rother's ACE alternative students, they will continue on with a new teacher. Rother writes, "I will remain connected as advisor-coordinator and hope to get into the program physically as often as I can. . . . The ACE program will maintain its participation in the 'mediACEnter' and affiliated activities. It would kill me to see ACE wither and die."

Chapter 7

NEW LITERACIES AND HIGH SCHOOL ENGLISH

Profile: Heather Harrigan, Richard Merkel, Cathy Yusep, and the English Department of Bowness High School Calgary, Alberta

In sprawling Calgary, I found a well-developed system for teaching new literacies within a standardized test–driven environment. This system was developed collaboratively over a period of years by several teachers in the English Department who got together on Friday afternoons to talk. One of the first things they decided was that, in the English Department at Bowness High School, the emphasis would be squarely on "text," no matter what form it takes, and these texts would include hairstyles, interior designs, and even cherry pies. "There is no text that should be ignored," stated department chair Heather Harrigan. Indeed, what sold me on visiting Bowness High School occurred during my phone interview with Harrigan, when she shared that some of her students had recently performed an interpretive dance in response to a text they had read (a dance that they performed for me when I visited). Harrigan also described an assignment in which students considered the symbolic meaning of flowers and were asked to create a bouquet or wreath for one of the characters in the play *Hamlet.* In another assignment, students were asked to re-create a famous writer's "writing room," including details that would reflect the life and times of the author when he or she was writing. Students were to create at least one of the objects from the room as an artifact, although this artifact could be created virtually. Harrigan kept rattling off these innovative assignments that were developed or researched by her entire English Department. In addition, it appeared that students were concurrently responding and thinking about such disparate text creators as Langston Hughes, Thomas Hardy, Tim Burton, Don McLean, and Frida Kahlo. And they were doing all this in English class.

While not all students at the school take advantage of the opportunity to work in new literacies, those choices are made explicitly available, in an organizational framework that allows for and encourages these choices while still functioning in a grade-based, standardized test–assessed school. These teachers have answered the dilemma: "I would like to do more 'new literacies,' but I don't know how to incorporate it into a standards-driven, print-centric curriculum." Alberta has a provincial test that all students must take at the end of Grade 12. And Bowness students do well on this test, with a student passing rate regularly in the 90% range (although the passing cutoff score is 50%). Students do well on the provincial exams even after having taken English classes that look at multiple forms of texts both personally and critically.

In addition to multiliterate classrooms, nestled close to the beautiful Canadian Rockies and the breathtaking Banff and Lake Louise, I found one of the most intensely collaborative high school English departments I have ever seen. There have been hurt feelings along the way, and, to their credit, the teachers make no attempt to hide the controversies that have existed over the years as their philosophy has been implemented. There have been some teachers who have transferred to other schools within the Calgary City Schools. Still, they keep talking about teaching and learning.

I found myself shivering on Harrigan's back porch. In May, it was still chilly, but many of the teachers were in T-shirts and tank tops as we chowed down on some Alberta beef. I think I gained 10 pounds during the 5 days I spent in Alberta, and this was because they apparently believe that the staff that eats together stays together. In fact, most of the teachers eat lunch at school around a very large table placed squarely in the middle of the small English Department office. The dialogue at these lunches reminded me of the lunchroom scenes from the British television comedy *Are You Being Served?* The challenges of teaching and collaborating have not always been easy for this group of teachers, but most of them manage to eat together and laugh together.

THE SCHOOL AND THE CURRICULUM

Bowness High School has 1,300 students and, while nondiverse racially, is quite diverse socioeconomically with only 15 to 20% of students going on to college. Formerly led by now-retired department chair Richard Merkel and succeeded by current chair Heather Harrigan, this department has worked through its commitment to multiliteracies. They have been greatly aided by teacher-librarian Cathy Yusep from whom I discovered this English department, through a nomination from an electronic mailing list (http://email.rutgers.edu/archives/child_lit.html). Whereas some of the other classrooms profiled in this book were obviously led by one to three teachers or by a single librarian, this curriculum design seemed to be truly a team effort, and one that clearly spilled over into the private lives of the Bowness High School English Department. The day I arrived, the department was accepting a Celebrating Innovative Practice Award from the Calgary Regional Association for Supervision and Curriculum Development (ASCD).

Over the few days that I visited Calgary, I listened to these teachers talk about the process they followed while writing their new literacies curriculum. As Harrigan described the beginnings, many of the English teachers had come from other schools, but when they got to Bowness, they found that they had a high percentage of failures in some of their classes. About 6 years ago, the teachers began talking and wondering why they were not being successful with some of their students. The group of teachers began to get together after school on Fridays to read and talk. They began asking themselves, "What do we believe about learning and teaching?" They created a two-column chart that they began to fill in. In our ideal school, they asked, what should we see "more of" and what should we see "less of"? The teachers came up with a list of things they would want to see "less of": "Teacher-directed learning; mystery learning; teacher as God; no 'full frontal' teaching."

Richard Merkel reflected on their path:

> I go back, probably to 1992. I had personally always been troubled by the way that schools stream kids, and I was unsettled by the kinds of perceptions in students that streaming created for students about what they were and what they could be and their choices in life. And then, through fortuitous circumstances indeed, it so happened some people left the department that I was the leader in, [and] we were able to get people in who were

asking the same kinds of questions. Over the course of a number of years, we gradually began to build a team that allowed us
to have these informal conversations about the perceptions of
what these kids were, and then it broadened. . . . Originally, the
conversations were always about the "classroom from hell"—
the ones we didn't really want to go face, but the ones we duti-
fully did. So, it went from that to actually the deeper conversation about what were the beliefs about teaching and learning,
what should be motivating the practice that goes on in our
classrooms on a daily basis. As people new to the school and the
department came in, they brought that kind of wealth of experiences with the difficult classes. Plus, a lot of them had done a
lot of professional reading and that allowed us to make a conversation about the philosophy of learning and what learning
should be. What happened at a point in time is that we got a
critical mass of people who wanted to have this conversation.
And over lunch hours over a period of time it became the topic
of conversation. We just ate lunch, and we actually talked about
what teaching and learning should look like; we tried to come
to an idea about what kinds of principles should underpin that
kind of practice in the classroom. We went from that kind of
informal conversation to a more active kind of planning and
talking. . . . "Well, what would this look like in the classroom?"
"How would we have to change what we do, not just in terms
of teaching of the materials, but actually in the structure of the
classroom, and in the structure of the department?"

The teachers also invited outsiders, such as local principals and a
professor from the University of Calgary, to their Friday meetings to
get their input. "To make sure we weren't just steamrolling the
process," said Merkel, "we listened carefully to people who thought
what we were trying to do wouldn't work, or [that it] wasn't in the
best interests of students." Much of the decision making centered
around the teachers' increasing inclination to "de-track" or "de-
stream" their classes, putting students of all abilities together in all
English classes. Eventually, they decided to begin enacting their plans
at the 10th-grade level. Teacher Karen Pegler remembered the importance of talk among the teachers in developing this new curriculum
and instruction: "I remember just talking and talking and talking during lunch hours, after school. And then to begin the talk, to begin the
professional dialogue, it did start from frustration. I know I had a
grade 10 nonacademic class and 19 out of 34 students were repeating

the course." Retired teacher Deanna Hunt said,

> You have to be able to subjugate what you normally do and not
> just say, well this is the way I've always done it. Because that's
> what all the talk was about—well, how else can this be done
> and what can we all agree on. That was a slow process, because
> there was a number of people who really felt in their hearts that
> was the way they wanted to go. But if you were willing to take
> that chance and talk to other people and to work together, it
> was quite an interesting process.

A key part of their collaboration was that they were joined by a
teacher-librarian, Cathy Yusep. The title that librarians carry in this
district is "Teacher-Librarian," because they are expected to be teachers as well as librarians. Yusep explained,

> The role of the teacher-librarian is to be involved as a team
> member, collaboratively planning and to be right in there and
> one of the teachers. The library, the physical space, is an exten-
> sion of the classroom. You cannot break it away from any of the
> other classrooms, and it's not just the English classroom, it's all
> of the classrooms in school. It's sort of an organic and flexible
> feeling, and if that doesn't occur, then it's a barrier to the kind
> of learning that we're talking about here.

Harrigan described what they want to see more of:

> We'll . . . see more of students constructing their own essential
> questions. We'll see them making choices about how they
> demonstrate what they understand. We'll see teachers facilitat-
> ing talk and teachers having metacognitive conversations with
> students. So when a student says, "Well, I don't get this text,"
> instead of saying, "Well let me explain that to you," saying
> "OK, what strategies have you used to understand it?" And
> "What strategies can you use that you haven't tried to under-
> stand it?"

Their inspiration for allowing students to not be so print-based was
assessment, based on their readings of Howard Gardner (1983, 1993,
1995). Harrigan related, "The guys we've been reading say if we're
going to understand broad-based assessment, if we're going to value
the different ways the students can demonstrate what they understand, then we better get out of print."

The teachers took about a year of reading and discussing, reading and discussing. After this, they determined that they had some core beliefs:

- All students can learn.
- All learning is readiness.
- The teacher's job is to provide understanding in a variety of ways.
- All text is equal.
- Text is anything that communicates—"A garden is a text."

One of the things the department wanted to see was an increase in instruction that was student driven. "We become successful in our jobs when we are redundant," stated Harrigan. "So when our Grade 12s are saying to us 'We'll let you know if we need you,' we say 'Gottcha!, All right, that's good!' because we're not going out there [in the real world] with them. They're going out there without us."

In this era of increasing reliance on standardized tests, it was amazing to hear the teachers talking about school reform that depended on student choice. Former assistant principal Linda Davis commented:

[This English program is] innovative on a number of fronts. The whole department is involved, so all students in Grades 10, 11, and 12 are involved in the program. Then you look at things like, this is a program that really involves the student and the student has to take a bigger role in their own education more than they do in other programs. So when you go in some classes, and you basically open up and take notes, pour it in, stuff it in, regurgitate it out, this is different. Now the students have to come up with their own ideas about what they think. They have to rethink those ideas; they have to process them in a variety of manners. They have numerous presentations around a variety of ways of doing things.

The teachers wanted this student independence partly because they also wanted a "blended" program in which college-bound students were in the same class with non-college-bound students. Harrigan stated,

If we're going to teach in a blended program, we have to make sure that we give all of the strategies to our students that they need to be successful. No student fails our course because of ability, ever! Because that's a failure on the teacher's part to provide the learning that that student needed. They fail it because they don't hand things in, never because of ability.

So the Bowness English teachers do not track students in any way in the 10th and 11th grades—it is a blended program (see Figure 7.1). They do track students in Grade 12, because the end-of-year provincial exams are either for college-prep or non-college-prep students. How the student does on this provincial exam counts for 50 percent of his or her overall grade for the course.

STRUCTURE: FIRST LOOKS, SEMINARS, AND SECOND LOOKS

The Bowness English Department teachers devised a format (see Figure 7.2) that includes what they call First Looks, Seminars, and Second Looks. They are not exactly sure who came up with the terms *First Look* and *Second Look*, but they attribute them to Kathleen Jones, a former Calgary English teacher who is now an administrator with Calgary Schools. This format would be followed in all of the English classes at the school.

In the first step of this process, students are given a general outline of the course (see Figure 7.3) as well as a list of texts focusing on the first essential question to be examined. Students are to select between four and six of these texts to read on their own and write a response to. These are the First Looks. The students are then placed in heterogenous small groups of four to six students, where they discuss their First Looks. This is called the First Seminar. During this First Seminar, the group decides upon three of the texts that they feel best help them to understand the essential question. Students in the group who have not read these three texts are then expected to read them on their own and provide First Looks to these texts.

Then, the group reconvenes for its Second Seminar, in which students discuss the three texts further, either starting with details found in the texts and then going to the larger essential question, or starting with the essential question and going to the details found in the texts. By the end of this process, students are expected to understand the text creator's intention and how it has addressed the essential question, what purposeful strategies the text creator has used to address the essential question, and what further essential questions are suggested by these works. They do this in the form of a Second Look around all three of the texts, which students do independently,

FIGURE 7.1 Overview of English Program at Bowness High School

- Grade 10 and Grade 11 courses are blended for all English language arts students in the school.
- All students study the same program.
- Grade 11 program builds on the Grade 10 program.
- Differentiation occurs in content, process, and product.
- Learning is driven by multiple literacies, with a broadened definition of text (includes works of literature and other texts in oral, print, visual, and multimedia forms).
- Emphasis is on metacognition (thinking about thinking). Metacognition involves reflection, self-awareness, and recognition of strategies employed and assessing the effectiveness of skills and strategies.
- Emphasis is on student choice.

and they may do this in any format. If students compose this Second Look in a nonprint medium, they must write a print rationale for the choices they made as they were creating their Second Look. Finally, each group selects one of their three texts and presents it to the entire class. This presentation may be in any text form in which they choose, again demonstrating how the text author has dealt with the essential question. All during the process, students are graded on both their individual work and their collaborative work.

During the first reading process, while students are composing their First Looks, they are instructed to record any felt "cognitive dissonance." "We tell them 'understanding is in dissonance,'" related Harrigan. "We have set up a response process that students go through, and that process is designed to help them understand metacognitively how we understand a text—that we begin from the personal, and we have to work our way through to the critical." It is during the Second Looks that the teachers see students moving toward a more critical response, with the Second Looks coming out of the talk that occurs during the seminars, talk that is designed to critically examine the author's purpose and the author's perspective on the essential question. See Figure 7.4 for a rubric that the teachers use to assess Second Looks. (Criteria can be added for an individual student to work on, thus allowing for differentiated instruction.)

When it comes time to assign a course grade, students also do a self-assessment that is added to by teachers (see Figure 7.5). These self-assessments are based on goals and how much growth the student has demonstrated toward reaching those goals. Students' First Looks and Second Looks are also graded by the teacher, as is the stu-

FIGURE 7.2 English Department Format at Bowness High School

1. Students are given a calendar (which is really a syllabus).
2. Students are given titles of 15–20 texts related to an "essential question." Each student is to choose 4–6 of them to write "First Looks" about.
3. Students get into heterogenous small groups and discuss the texts they have read. This is called "First Seminar."
4. The group decides on the three texts that best answer or deal with the essential question. Students who have not read these texts are to go back and read them and write First Looks about them.
5. The group comes back together for a "Second Seminar" in which they discuss the three texts more specifically—how does the author deal, in detail, with the essential question?
6. Students are to then write "Second Looks" about each of the three texts, in response to the discussion they have had.
7. Each group presents one text to the entire class. This presentation consists of the students commenting on how the text deals with the essential question. This presentation can be in any medium.

dents' performance in one or more Seminars. "[The rubric] has to do with what it is to be a learner, what it looks like to be a learner," stated Harrigan. "And it doesn't say that you have to be good at these things; it says that you have to embrace these things."

USING NEW LITERACIES

The days I visited the Bowness English Department classes, I saw a traditional, print-based curriculum infused with new literacies choices. It was clearly understood that teachers are expected to prepare students for a provincial exam (diploma exam) that includes such literary terms as: allegory, allusion, analogy, anecdote, apostrophe (the figure of speech), cacophony, caricature, irony, oxymoron, simile, metaphor, and synecdoche. Students are also expected to write essays on the exam. Essay topics over the years have included asking students to explore themes such as the following:

- An author's treatment of the ways in which individuals respond to challenge
- The basis for and the impact of individual choices
- The factors that contribute to and result from an individual's desire to escape
- Individual responses to significant dilemmas

- Human isolation and its effect on individuals
- An individual's response to challenge
- An individual's ability to adapt to situations in life

While the required passing rate for the province is relatively low (50%), the Bowness High School English Department got 100 percent of its graduating seniors to that level. Approximately one week before the exam, the English Department attempts to get the students ready for the provincial exam by teaching test-taking skills specific to the format of the exam.

Still, even in this standardized paper-and-pencil test environment, I saw a variety of assignments being used in the English classes I observed that asked students to read and write in a variety of forms of representation. In one assignment, students were to pick one scene from a film such as *The Shawshank Redemption* (Darabont, 1994) or *The Mosquito Coast* (Weir, 1986) and compare it to a scene from a print text such as *Romeo and Juliet*. Students were to "describe the scene's use of color, dialogue, sound, action and lighting and how these components work together to create an impact." Students were then to draw the scene they selected from the film and draw the scene selected from the print text. Finally, students were to "consider [the scene's] impact emotionally and intellectually," and "compare and contrast [their] reactions to the viewed image and the written text."

To get students used to looking at the deeper meaning of images, the teachers would ask the students to respond to painting such as "What I Saw in the Water" by Frida Kahlo (see Figure 7.6). Once students are used to studying visuals, they are encouraged to translate a character from a print text into a visual. By using the RAFTS template, the teachers are attempting to teach that such considerations as audience and topic mustbe considered by creators in all media.

Non-print-based projects were sometimes used by the teachers to get at underlying meanings of print texts. For example, the main point of the Art Trading Card assignment, created by teacher Linda Bialek (see Figure 7.7), is, according to Harrigan, "to go beyond your literal understandings of the play and discuss at a metaphorical and symbolic level."

There were also instances in which students would choose an object such as a candle or jewelry box to represent ideas they had first encountered in print. Students were expected to write rationales for how an object such as a jewelry box, for example, could represent the themes in a poem by Amy Lowell.

The students in the English classes at Bowness were getting a

FIGURE 7.3 Sample English Course Outline

The English 30 course will focus on the language arts strands of reading, writing, listening, viewing, speaking, and representing. The concepts and skills developed will represent the outcomes from the Alberta Learning Program of Studies: exploring, understanding, managing information, creating, and collaborating. We will also be continuing our work to develop the metacognitive strategies necessary for continued growth and lifelong learning.

The Umbrella Question: *What Are the Questions That Have Shaped Our World?*

During our study of the umbrella question, we will study a variety of themes and essential questions.

Unit One: In What Way Do We Define the Boundaries of Our World?

Students will explore the umbrella question using a multitext approach. This will include short stories, film, video, poetry, and multimedia text.

Unit Two: What is the Individual's Role in Change?

Do individuals have any recourse when faced with great change in their worlds? In this unit, students will study and create a variety of texts including a modern play.

Unit Three: What is the Relationship Between Privilege and Responsibility?

Students will study and create a variety of texts including *Hamlet.* Students will also identify the enduring questions for study as they access, study, and create a variety of texts including short stories, Shakespeare, novels, poetry, modern plays, visuals, and multimedia.

Final Project: Students will be asked to reflect upon how the texts they have studied and created have helped them understand the umbrella question. This will involve a group and individual response.

Mark Distribution
Coursework: 90 %
Growth: 10%
This will constitute 50% of the student's overall average.
Alberta Learning Diploma Exam counts for 50%.of overall grade.

FIGURE 7.4 Rubric to Assess the Second Look

	Thought	*Detail*	*Presentation*
5: *Superior*	The student's created text and accompanying rationale demonstrate critical thinking, and an insightful exploration of the studied text.	The student's ideas are supported with purposefully chosen specific details and quotations from the original text. Explicit details establish a strong connection between the created text and the studied text.	The response is polished. Stylistic choices are effective. Grammar and spelling errors are relatively absent in the student's writing. The created text is carefully prepared. Student effort is impressive.
4: *Proficient*	The student's created text and accompanying rationale demonstrate critical thinking, and a thoughtful exploration of the studied text.	The student's ideas are supported with appropriate details from the original text. Relevant details establish a clear connection between the created text and the studied text.	The response is polished. Stylistic choices are considered. Grammar and spelling are considered in the student's writing. The created text is carefully prepared. Student effort is obvious.
3: *Satisfactory*	The student's created text and accompanying rationale demonstrate a literal interpretation and some critical thinking, and a general exploration of the studied text.	The student's ideas are supported with general details from the original text. Adequate details establish a straightforward connection between the created text and the studied text.	The response is polished. Grammar and spelling are considered, but more revision may be necessary in the student's writing. The created text demonstrates some care in preparation. Student effort is evident.
2: *Limited*	The student's created text and accompanying rationale are unclear or undeveloped. There is little or no exploration. The text demonstrates literal thinking.	The created text does not refer to the original text, or the reference is unclear or inappropriate. The connection between the created text and the studied text is unclear.	The response is not polished. Grammar and spelling errors are too frequent and reduce the quality of the student's writing. The created text does not demonstrate care. Student effort is minimal.
1: *Poor*	The response does not demonstrate an attempt to explore the studied text.	There is no connection between the studied text and the created text. The rationale may be absent.	There is little evidence of student effort. The created text may be sloppy, incomplete, or careless.

FIGURE 7.5 Student Self-Assessment for English Courses

Response Journal

Review Response Journal assignments for the four stories in the first unit of study. Review the rubric. Review the response to "What Sort of Learner Am I?" Comment on each of the following prompts. Be specific.
- Describe your exploring skills. How have they improved? In what way can they be improved?
- How much of the response journal is a plot summary? How much is devoted to exploring themes and ideas; elements of the story, like symbol, irony, and foreshadowing; how much personal or observed experience is included as part of the exploring process?
- How frequently are text-based details provided to support and clarify the conclusions you draw?
- To what extent do your polished Second Looks reflect your best effort? Do you edit, proofread, word process, format, other?
- On what one or two areas will you focus to improve?

Seminar

Comment on your contribution to the seminar. Clarify your thinking. Provide specific detail.
- Frequency: How often do you contribute to the discussion? How has the frequency changed over the period of several seminars?
- Content: Do you contribute ideas? Details? Ask questions? Bring problems for the group to help you solve? Are you able to contribute to the analysis of symbol, irony? How often do you contribute or make use of personal experience to clarify and support the discussion?
- Listening skills: Are you an active or passive listener? Do you support the ideas of fellow students? Do you help with the exploring process? Do you make eye contact? Do you encourage others to explore their ideas? Do you interrupt? Does your body language say you're interested?
- How prepared are you for the seminar? How often does the First Look meet expectations? How often does it exceed minimum expectation? Has a seminar been missed due to lack of preparation or forgetting the seminar date?

General Comments

Comment on each of the following questions. Be specific in answering.
- Are you able to keep up with the pace of the work?
- How do you feel you are doing at meeting the course expectations?
- How have your organizational skills changed and improved over the course of the first month? How are you using the Student Agenda?
- Have you set a regular study and homework time in the evening?
- How have you contributed to the learning of others?
- How many deadlines have you missed?
- How would someone know that you care about your work and are giving your best effort?
- How well do you use class time?

workout in how nonliteral representations can have meaning, no matter the medium. And they were getting practice in going from a personal to a critical response to these works, and writing about them in multiple forms, forming their responses both individually and collaboratively.

WHAT THE STUDENTS SAY

Students seemed particularly positive about the choices that they are given in the Bowness English Department. I asked to speak to randomly selected students who had failed English, and even these students were positive. Two students described an art project they did in response to watching the film *Edward Scissorhands* (Burton, 1990). Rhonda said:

We started out with a doll, because it's better to show what we're trying to express. It's better than just writing it, because with writing, people don't get the whole idea of what we're trying to do. So we just made a doll. It used to be a ballerina, but we made it creepy. Like all the colors, the red and the black, it's like pain and the shadows he lived in, and this is all the values that he taught the town which is in the movie.

Her partner Gina added: "This helps to visualize a lot of things. . . . We can kind of show what we are thinking." Another girl, Gloria, stated, "They don't give us a bunch of questions that we have to answer, and if we don't answer it, it's wrong. We get to interpret the movie however we see it and I guess they liked it, so it worked!"

Angela described how she responded to the film:

I did the same *Edward Scissorhands* project as them, only I interpreted it in a different way. I built a model to show how his life was. I answered my own essential question which was, "How does a person change society while being changed themselves?" I split [a] birdcage in half—so that it could represent who he was before he met society, and who he was after society. Inside there's things hanging to show what he cared about most. . . . He went down to the society; he discovered hands and how much he really wanted them. And he found things like love and betrayal, lies and things like that. He also found out, like what can happen to people and also what society is really like. I want-

FIGURE 7. 6 Frida Kahlo Prompt

Introduction

Frida Kahlo was an important artist of the twentieth century. Many of her paintings were about the people and events of her life. One of her paintings, _What I Saw in the Water_ combined a number of images from other paintings into one work. Take a close look at this work. Can you see the rim of a bathtub, the water, and someone's toes? How many images, or details, are there in and/or on the water? At this time, turn to the back side of the painting. Here are the individual works that Frida Kahlo chose to include. Examine each painting and its title. Taken together, they constitute a highly personal, pictorial history of the painter. What comment might she be making about her life? Why has she chosen some images and not others? Are the images linked or sequenced in any particular way? How do the images make you feel? What if the painting were about the main character/protagonist of the text you are now studying? What framing element (like a bathtub) might be chosen? What images? How would they be sequenced? What view of life would be communicated?

Task

For a main character of the text being studied, create a visual that illustrates the character's life. Choose images/details which the character might include, which taken together make a comment on the meaning of life from that character's perspective. The images/details may be real, like the toes and water in Kahlo's work, and/or surreal and fantastic, like the volcano or the seashell waterspout. All visuals should be contained within a framing element. Kahlo used the bathtub.

Evaluation

The final product will be marked according to the rubric. Value: 30 marks
Draft work must also be submitted for the product to be complete.
Process mark to be determined by the teacher.

RAFTS

The following are suggestions:
R = Role. The character you have selected.
A = Audience. Who would you expect to find meaning in this visual?
F = Format. See the model provided to guide you.
T = Topic. How does this visual reflect the soul of the character chosen?
S = Strong verb. What emotional response should this visual evoke in the viewer?

---

ed to show how society puts on a mask kind of. . . . I chose to do a birdcage—it shelters him; at the same time, he can't get out of it. He can never be free from the restraints that are put on it, but he can see what's out there. And so it's kind of his shelter

FIGURE 7.6 (continued)

Rubric

A superior text will:
   • Include a minimum of 8–10 events
   • Use color literally and symbolically
   • Show thoughtful use of composition elements: Foreground, midground, background, as well as top, middle, bottom; sequencing of ideas, focal point, scale of elements (proportion)
   • Have a literal or symbolic framing element
   • Include an explicit rationale explaining composition choices and the RAFT components

Note: Images may be gathered from a variety of sources and need not be hand drawn; however, images must be modified to suit RAFTs and arranged compositionally to conform to the rubric.

---

and his prison all at the same time. I thought that worked. I put a little mirror in there, with a hole cut straight through so he could see who he was and who he had turned into, representing the two sides, so he could always see himself, who he was.

Three girls described how and why they created an interpretive dance in response to a short story, "Happy Event" (1956) by Nadine Gordimer. In this story, a young black servant named Lena is arrested after apparently giving birth and leaving her baby to die in a ditch. While Lena's guilt is in question, Gordimer contrasts Lena's situation with that of her employer, Ella, a rich white woman who has just returned from safely having an abortion. The three students choreographed a dance in three parts. In the first part of the dance, one of the girls placed herself in a huge fabric bag and simulated a struggle to escape the bag. In the second part of the dance, one of the girls built a double-sided costume, one half of which represented Lena and one half representing Ella. The third part of the dance reenacted an interrogation in the story. One of the three students, Brittany, explained:

We're trying to attack [the character's] emotional moral boundaries, so we thought it was important to touch on all of them, to have an interesting visual with Cheryl [another student] in a

FIGURE 7.7 Art Trading Card Assignment

Grade 11—Macbeth

Art trading cards are playing card-sized pieces of art. You will reflect your under-standings of the play in your cards. You may use your imagination for the design and medium of your cards. For example, your card could use collage, crayon, crayon resist, felts, fabric, pencil crayons, paint, pastels. We will look at a selection of art trading cards to show you how the size of the card is not a limiting factor on what you can create! Here are some guidelines you must follow:

(a) You are going to use your responses to each scene to help you with this proj-ect. You may use your headlines, sketches, or summaries. You may use ideas you have already created or add and delete ideas. The main focus of this assignment is to go beyond your literal understandings of the play and discuss at a metaphorical and symbolic level.

(b) You will be including a rationale with your card in order to explain the choic-es you make. What are you showing? What understandings of the play are included in the card? Why is this important? Why did you choose the medi-um and design? What did you hope the viewer of the card would understand about your card and the play?

(c) There are some ideas you may want to consider in each act. The first act you may want to consider Macbeth's change of values. The second act you may focus on the question, "Expectations Met?" Act three is a great opportunity to look at Macbeth's change of character. Act IV and V provide you with a con-trast of who Macbeth is with who Macbeth was at the beginning of the play.

bag, stretching out and showing, kind of, if there was a bound-ary and you could see it, that's what it would be and then it shows the linking connection between the two women with the double-sided baby, and as I talk, I rotate, so you can see all sides so you see my back and you see that there is no face in the back, with the baby and then the white woman who's fully defined in the front, and then the side, where it's almost all one womb. We tried to touch on everything, and then with the interrogation, we try to touch on the morals and the personal boundaries that are set.

Her partner Courtney said:

Another reason we did the three [parts of the dance] is that they're so different. Multiple intelligences is a big thing in this program. Ever since Grade 10 you find out what your multiple intelligence is. And so people learn in different ways, and so we thought, if they could see a dance, [they'd see the] boundaries they're doing with whatever actions they take. For hers, you could visually see the one womb, even though they face in completely opposite directions. It's for the people with listening skills who need to hear people talking.

I asked Harrigan what she says in response to a criticism that having students make dolls and choreograph dances are "fluff" assignments. She responded vehemently:

Usually all I have to do is show a rationale to someone and say, "Show me the fluff in this!" Because the level of thinking that a student has done to create that text is quite a bit more analytical than any level of thinking they would do simply by doing a test or some short answer thing or an essay. It takes incredible skill of thinking, critical thinking to create what they create; for example, our Grade 12s just finished doing a project on *Hamlet*—Act IV. So we said, "create a bouquet" for Ophelia. Now, in order to do that, they have to understand that character, they have to know how flowers in that time were representative of particular feelings, and they have to put something together that is symbolic of that character, of what happened with her. They have to make some choices about . . . that the writer of the play did not make. Did she kill herself? They have to do that and create it. And then they have to write a rationale explaining all of the purposeful choices they made. As far as I'm concerned, the skills required in doing that are much more analytical than the skills required in most of the traditional work that we ask students to do.

I was able to see many rationales done by students. One student described why he designed his *Macbeth* art card in the way he did:

My card for the first act of *Macbeth* has many different images arrayed on it in a collage format. The images that I chose all represent an event or idea that occurred in the first act of this play. The

central image of one that jumps out at you the most is that of
Macbeth on a marionette string. I chose to depict him as a control-
lable puppet because his wife forces him into killing Duncan.

Another student wrote:

For this trading card, I tried to show a number of different
things about the first act of *Macbeth.* One of the first things
that a person might notice when looking at the card is the background. It is half-black, half-white, which is divided by a cut
line down the middle. This was shown in order to portray
Macbeth's change of values in the play.

Another student depicted Macbeth descending a staircase and wrote:
"I wanted to show that Macbeth's values change as each scene develops, through the depicted stages of each stair on the staircase. As
Macbeth walks down each step, it's like he develops his evil side
heading toward the goals led out to him by Lady Macbeth."

As an example of one of these rationales, I read one from a student who had taken a jewelry box and ornately decorated it with
bright red paper, sequins, and special ribbons. This was in response to
a poem by Amy Lowell called "Patterns."

The poem Patterns was about a lady during the seventeenth-
eighteenth century who was looking for love to unlock her true
identity. The red sequined heart box is to represent the heart
and emotions of the lady in the poem. The box is red to signify
love and passion. It became evident that the woman was full of
passion that she could not identify or reveal—"For my passion
wars against the stiff brocade."—The red represents that the
passion is there and is connected to love. The heart is very ele-
gant because that is how I pictured the lady. She had a regal feel
about her. The heart box is surrounded by a chain and a lock.
This signifies how her love and passion were locked away and
hidden. When you unhook the heart, shedding the chain, you
are left with a box to which the contents are unknown. Inside
the box are flowers in a bed of cotton—"Underneath my stiff-
ened gown is the softness of a woman bathing in a marble
basin." The cotton represents the softness that the chains would
not reveal. There are flowers in her heart because flowers in the
poem were an important symbol of the type of person she wanted to be—"The daffodils and squills flutter in the breeze as they

please—and I weep." I thought that she was a flower inside (soft, loving, tender, beautiful) and one was weeping because the flower could not survive in her heart for so long. The flowers needed sunlight—not to be hidden away.

There are many more rationales I could quote, demonstrating Bowness students' abilities to translate meaning from text form to text form. After spending several days with this intensely collaborative staff, I came away with a vision of new literacies that is centered on choices and options and is in response to student and teacher needs. Second-year teacher Sarah Nordean summed up the nature of the department's curriculum journey: "I teach with a team of teachers—some are veterans; some are as inexperienced as I am. We all plan and learn from each other. . . . As a department we are constantly working together to make new literacies a strong part of our program. . . . In fact, our department essentially uses new literacies as an approach to program development."

As Yusep, the teacher-librarian stated, "I came here and saw that these teachers, they don't teach English. They teach kids. They teach students. And that is a crucial difference."

Chapter 8

FINAL THOUGHTS: "MY GRANDCHILDREN'S TIME ZONE"

I set out to find teachers who are actually trying to teach new literacies on a daily basis. As it turned out, I have found new literacies in different kinds of schools and for different reasons: in rural settings (Snow Lake) and urban (San Fernando and Parma); in college-prep classes (Parma and Peacock); and in an alternative school (Lake of Two Mountains). These efforts were led by the school librarian (Peacock); by an English department (Bowness); by an interdisciplinary team of teachers (Parma); and by lone teachers (Lake of Two Mountains and Snow Lake). They were dominated by technology (Snow Lake, Peacock, and Lake of Two Mountains) and not dominated by technology (Parma and Bowness). They were undertaken for critical literacy purposes (Snow Lake, San Fernando, and Bowness) and for more arts-driven, aesthetic reasons (Parma and Bowness); and they intended to achieve goals of student personal empowerment (Lake of Two Mountains, Snow Lake, San Fernando, Bowness, and Parma) and to support the teaching of content (Parma, Peacock, and Bowness). They were included in programs that are dependent on the passion of the teachers (Parma, Snow Lake, and Lake of Two Mountains) and in more systemic programs that perhaps will survive teacher turnover (Peacock and Bowness); in classrooms that are dominated more by film and television media (Lake of Two Mountains and San Fernando), ones that are dominated more by visual art and music (Bowness and Parma), and ones that are dominated by software (Snow Lake and Peacock). Most of these classrooms, however, are combinations of several different rationales and approaches.

The reader of this book may be surprised that I neglected one source or another for finding these classrooms; I don't doubt that there are classrooms out there that "do" new literacies much more effectively than one or more of the teachers profiled in this book. Some readers may also think, "I've been doing that for years!" or "The person who teaches next door to me does that!" I would submit that the kinds of projects described in this book are stand-ins for the many pioneers of new literacies at the turn of this century. What I am doing is naming these novel but burgeoning activities as belonging under the new literacies umbrella. I believe the teachers profiled in this book provide us with snapshots of what the evolving literacy classroom looks like at the beginning of the twenty-first century in North America, at a time when teachers themselves are grappling with the great digital revolution that has taken us in 25 years from the balcony of the Summit Mall Cinema to high-speed internet delivery of films. The teachers profiled in this book may not be aware of all the pedagogical theory surrounding multiliteracies, but they are part of the vanguard of educators who are both creating and reflecting the evolution of literacy in education.

TRENDS OF THE DATA

As I examined the data obtained from the classroom visits, I kept noticing a tension coming through as a result, perhaps, of being part of this vanguard. Often, as I observed in these classrooms, the goals of new literacies teachers and students seemed conflicted. What was the point? Was the point to give students ways of expressing themselves that they had not previously been able to utilize? Was the purpose to teach kids to use PowerPoint and Flash so they could be more employable in the future? Or were these goals necessarily mutually exclusive? Were new literacies often used to promote a new autonomous version of literacy? As Street (1995) had described, the "autonomous" model of print literacy had assumed that illiterates would autonomously take great steps into light out of darkness when they learned to read. "According to this 'great divide' theory," Street wrote, "'illiterates' are fundamentally different from literates" (p. 21). On the other hand, according to Street, those who subscribe to an "ideological" model of literacy "concentrate on the specific social practices of reading writing, . . . [recognizing] the ideological and therefore culturally embedded nature of such practices" (p. 29). So, after seeing all the students who speak about stepping into the light of learning Flash animation, perhaps they and their teachers are buying into an autonomous model of new literacies. Have many of them, in fact, missed the point of these new literacies? Were these students being helped to use new literacies to make meaning for themselves or to make meaning out of the district's curriculum "standards" so that they could eventually get good jobs?

There were instances in which students were working on projects that came out of their own communities and themselves—Connie's sweatshop video in San Fernando, for example, or the Herb Lake ghost town website from Clarence Fisher's students in Snow Lake. Also, students frequently mentioned that utilizing non-print-based media helped them understand more about their own emotions. As quoted earlier, Lee Rother of Lake of Two Mountains High School saw his students as being mute before encountering new literacies. Fisher described how he wanted his students to be able to "design spaces to make meaning for themselves."

Still, it was frequently mentioned by students in all the settings that these new literacies skills, particularly when related to technology, were seen as mainly beneficial to their future job-seeking skills. Sometimes the students would express the feeling that they were on the wrong side of the digital divide. The students in Snow Lake, for example, talked about how they simply couldn't do things at home on their computers that they would like to do, due to slowness of their home equipment. Even in the non-technology-dominated Parma classroom, students commented that the class prepared them well for the job market. Students also mentioned that the collaborative nature of these classes prepared them well for the world of work. So were these classrooms, in the students' eyes, mainly there to prep them for the new economy (Gee, 2002, 2000b; Young, Dillon, & Moje, 2002)? In each data category, there were tensions evident between the freeing nature of these classrooms and the strain to exist in the current K–12 world of standardized tests and report cards.

Collaboration and Motivation

The emphasis on collaboration I witnessed in these classrooms was clear, but could be interpreted in different ways: Were teachers stressing the social nature of literacy, or were they just getting kids ready to be part of a "quality circle" out in the work world? Some teachers saw the collaborative nature of these assignments as of personal benefit to students. Nancy Krefetz, from Peacock Middle School, stated:

It took a lot of cooperation, and it was very, very difficult for them. Very difficult. . . . But I find, you know, especially at this age, they have to learn to work together; they have to learn to make decisions; and so it's not only, "What is an atom made of?" It's also your character. . . . I just think it's overall, you know, what it does for the human being—they learn technology; they learn to think critically; they have to cooperate; they have to learn to solve their own problems.

In every classroom studied, there were many group projects assigned. The SFETT classroom at San Fernando High was set up specifically to have computers facing each other rather than in rows up against a wall. The emphasis there was actually more on the process of collaboration than it was on using new literacies. In most of the classrooms profiled, in fact, the final grade assigned for the project was based equally, if not more, on the process of creating the product as well as on the product itself. Many of the classrooms included "time management" and "group skills" in their grading.

Many of the large Snow Lake projects were collaborative in nature. These students seemed quite adept at working in groups, perhaps because they had already been forced to work together for years due to their geographic isolation. When I asked one of the Snow Lake students what they would do when in a group that couldn't get along, he said, "We just go our separate ways. . . . We just split up for a few minutes." At Bowness, the entire structure of the English department was built around group seminars. In some cases, this was because teachers explicitly believed in the social nature of literacy. Heather Harrigan, of Bowness High, said, "They always work together and collaborate through it even when they're doing individual projects, because learning doesn't happen in isolation, you need to be able to turn to your buddy and say, 'What have you got for this?' because that's how we learn. We talk with others."

Out of this collaborative atmosphere may come a greater understanding of tolerance for some students. A student at Peacock Middle School talked about how these types of assignments allow for special needs students to participate. Colin, from Arts Seminar at Parma High, singled out learning how to work with others as one of the main things he got out of the class. One fellow Parma student, Hal, even singled out this type of teaching as having even more potential for improving the general level of tolerance in the high school.

Also out of this collaborative spirit may come a strengthened collective voice and an ability to reach out and communicate beyond the boundaries of the classroom. Many of the students at San Fernando High, for example, expressed a perceived lack of voice in their community and felt that SFETT and the collaboratively run ican Film Festival had given them more of a sense of agency. When I questioned Connie about why she wanted to be an education major, she said, "We want to make sure that the kids have a voice here and everywhere else they go. The skills that we learn here, the communication skills, the presenting skills, the planning skills [are] all necessary. . . . We know how to plan our papers or our presentations. We're not going to be shy anymore."

Making collaborative multimedia projects is a way for Connie and the other students to send out powerful messages to their own community and to the world, "even though we're only high school students." That's why they don't waste time doing videos on skateboarding. Interestingly, in two of the settings studied—Torres's in San Fernando and Rother's in Deux Montagnes—students were actually starting their own businesses related to media. They were working together to provide services to the community immediately.

The question still is there, however: Were these collaborative projects designed to get the students ready for the "world of work," or were there other reasons for their collaborative nature, such as a social view of literacy or the human need to balance individual and collaborative endeavors (John-Steiner, 1997)?

Multiple Text Forms

One of the main characteristics of these classrooms was allowing students to use multiple forms of representation on a daily basis. But were these new literacies seen as mainly motivational tools? Often the teachers would speak of using new literacies to motivate students, and several of the teachers used multiliteracies to reach at-risk students. Many of the students spoke of how boring traditional classrooms are. In contrast, teacher Veronica Marek at San Fernando High described how involving the new literacies activities are:

> These kids will come in here before the bell rings. They'll sit down. They'll start working. You know, you don't have to say, you know, turn on the computer, go here. They're already there. And when the bell rings, they're still working. And I've seen a lot of kids who have never stayed after school . . . stay after school to finish a project.

Barry, a student in Arts Seminar at Parma, described being motivated to learn about Sir Francis Bacon and Michel de Montaigne as his group gave a presentation pitting the philosophies of these two thinkers against each other in the style of a World Wrestling Federation (WWF) match. "[We] did a speech on the philosophies of Francis Bacon, Michel De Montaigne, and Absolutism. And we had to talk about those, and we turned it into a WWF-style kind of presentation."

In several of the new literacies classrooms in this study, alternative media were seen as tools that teachers could use to help teach content. Several students in the study said that they were "visual learners," but when pressed to explain how they know they are visual learners, they were unable to point to any kind of diagnostic test or assessment that they have gone through to show they are visual learners. They just seem to feel that they are better able to connect with the content of a course via alternative media. Some of the students from Peacock Middle School made the point that they felt they learned the content better working in new literacies because, in getting a product ready for completion, they had frequently to retype the text or remanipulate the content in some manner, so that by the time the project was fully assembled the content had virtually been memorized.

But does this emphasis force nonprint representations into a system in which ultimately symbols must return to verbal/written language in order to signify what they "really mean"? The only places I saw students creating without having to give "rationales" were San Fernando High School and Lake of Two Mountains High School, and even there many of the student videos still made extensive use of what were called in silent film days "title cards," which basically explained the intent of the video using English or Spanish. Are new literacies simply serving the "old" literacy of print?

I noticed frequently that even in these new literacies classrooms, print was still privileged as a form of representation. Students would need to provide a rationale in the form of print for a nonprint assignment. This print rationalization could be in the form of a written "rationale" justifying choices made in completion of a nonprint assignment, or the rationalization could be in the form of a "chain of evidence" that the student had followed in doing a research-based project. But, ultimately, the student had to get back to print.

A common assignment was for students to "translate" a text into another text. In the case of the Monument Project at Parma, students were to translate the entire life of a twentieth-century artist or writer into an abstract monument. At Bowness, students often would trans-

late a poem or a film into an abstract or representational object as
well, or they might have to translate an abstract artwork into print;
or, if it wasn't an exact translation, it was their own response mixed
in with a representation of the first text. At Snow Lake, Fisher
assigned students to make Flash animations of poetry (their own or
classic poems).

Most, if not all, of the teachers profiled in this book use the word
text when communicating with their students. Fisher discussed and
even had posters hanging in his room to the effect that "information
can be encoded in a number of symbol systems that all have 'rules'
that we agree on and that they must consciously understand these
rules, and call upon a known set of skills in order to fully comprehend the message that is being presented to them." Students were
able to speak on a sophisticated level of the characteristics of composing in PowerPoint or video. At San Fernando, students were indoc-
trinated that preplanning was the most important step of all in the
creative process, and this planning was to be done on paper.

Robert, of Lake of Two Mountains, didn't see much of a difference
in text forms:

> I do not see a difference between reading a book or reading a
> movie because when you're reading a book, you have to, you
> look at the words, and you get images in your head, like an idea
> of how it's going. When you're reading a video, you still have to
> look . . . it's like reading it. And you have to process it in your
> head to see how it is. It just makes you understand. I don't real-
> ly see a difference.

When I asked if writing in an alternative form isn't different, Robert
answered: "Well, you still have to have ideas. But instead of writing
it, like using a camera, for instance, you can just film things and
that's like writing. I still don't see a difference. It all still goes in the
same way into your head, and you just use it the way you look at it.
I don't really see a difference."

It was clear, however, that in most of these classrooms, I saw a
balance of reading nonprint media and writing in nonprint media,
although certain classrooms tended more toward writing (San
Fernando). As Fisher pointed out, becoming writers in nonprint
media can make students better readers of nonprint media (which
comes as no surprise to teachers of print literacy). "When they work
as producers of this kind of work," Fisher said, "it takes a lot of the
magic out of it for them. And they're no longer in awe of just the

flashy colors and I think a lot of that actually helps them concentrate on what's actually there instead of being in awe of all the colors and the animation." Still, in the classrooms I observed, to really convey what they had learned, students were often constrained to return ultimately to the medium of print.

A New Space for Teaching and Learning—Blurring the Lines

Perhaps in the end, however, these classrooms became transcendent places in spite of themselves. In spite of somewhat murky goals for collaboration and an ultimate reliance on print media, it was in the daily application of new literacies teaching and learning that such elements of the traditional classroom as time and traditional teacher-student roles became irrelevant—at least to the students. Students would often tell me that they had lost track of time in these classes. In San Fernando's SFETT, it became almost embarrassingly irrelevant and so "twentieth-century" to ask about course credit for the work the students were doing. It was the teachers who sometimes seemed to struggle with how to fit what they were doing into the organiza- *same as Bob* tionally designed assessment constraints of the school. Rother, of Lake of Two Mountains, actually said he didn't like rubrics because he found even those to be constraining. The only element that Torres and Marek "graded" in San Fernando was the process. Other teachers in this book held on to the expectations of the 5-point scale (A-B-C-D-F) and the need to prepare students for standardized tests.

Teachers spoke of having to let go of some of their preconceived "teacher" notions. Several spoke of having to let go of their conception of time. Students needed more time at various stages of these kinds of projects. "It is very difficult, as a high school teacher, not to think in terms of 'This is a 2-week unit no matter what happens,'" said Rich Zasa of Parma. Only Clarence Fisher, working in a self-contained classroom at Snow Lake, could fully let go, letting projects take as long or as short a time as needed. Teachers also talked about how it was difficult for them to let go of telling students the "right answer." From Parma, Rich Zasa says, "It really does run counter to *role of teacher learning* everything that you assume you should be doing as a teacher—that you should be controlling the process and the outcome. Because . . . you just really never know what's going to happen and where you're going to go and where the holes are." Bill Peck from Parma talks about a former student that used to beg them to just tell them what the right answer was.

Even if there were not explicit discussions of power and the way texts position us, these classrooms often positioned the students in more powerful positions within the classroom itself, and this was a difficult and lonely choice for these teachers to make. While students were being immersed in content via new literacies, many spoke of the space and freedom they felt in these classrooms, the space to feel emotions and to express themselves with a fluency they could not attain in conventional classrooms. As mentioned, the term *letting go* came up several times when talking with the teachers profiled in this book. This letting go included letting go of preconceived notions and old ways, teacher control of projects, traditional forms of assessment, traditional notions of time, and always having to have the right answer. Zasa of Parma High expressed some difficulty at letting go of more traditional paper-and-pencil forms of assessment: "As an English teacher, I kept thinking, 'If they don't write about it, they don't understand it.'"

One of the most striking themes to emerge from the data was a frequent reference to emotion on the part of students and teachers. Students would say that they learned about their own emotions and those of others in these classes. Gary, from Parma High, said that he had learned about emotions from working on the Monument Project, by working on principles of abstraction. I asked him how learning about abstraction helped him understand emotion better. He responded, "Say we go to an art museum, and we look at an abstract statue, we can understand through the artist what he was trying to portray. Like if there's sharp pointy spikes, we can understand maybe he was angry at something. Or if it was round, he was in a soft, more mellow mood."

There were also kids who said that there were certain things they could say using nonprint media that they couldn't say in print, that print was somehow constricting, and that one couldn't possibly say everything one wanted to in print. Said Rhonda, from Bowness: "We started out with a doll, because it's better to show what we're trying to express. It's better than just writing it, because with writing, people don't get the whole idea of what we're trying to do." Gina added, "This helps to visualize a lot of things. It gives us a chance to express what you're thinking without having to worry about questions and writing it all out. We can kind of show what we are thinking."

Jennifer, also from Bowness High, talked about how working in alternative media helps her to express emotions more accurately than if she were working with words:

I think it's really important to be using other forms of response

other than just writing out what you think about a piece of literature. Things like a poem really have emotion and you can
interpret them in a lot of different ways, and when you're
encouraged in a program to use the different mediums, then I
think you can open up what you're trying to express. Like you
don't have to put it into words. 'Cause if I was trying to explain
what I was trying to present and write it out, it wouldn't be
nearly as effective; I think I was trying to get across what I was
trying to get across through this. . . . We don't live in the written world.

Perhaps because of this difference from other classrooms that students perceived—a difference in fluency, a difference in visualization—students also seemed deeply conflicted over whether these new
literacies classrooms were "easy" or "hard." This easy-hard binary
manifested itself in student comments such as from students who
expressed that the new literacies class was "an easy A," yet would
also comment on the number of hours that were spent engrossed in
the project, working after school. It's sad to realize that, after a life-
time of traditional schooling, students may have been confusing
engagement with fluff. To them, for something to be "hard," it must
necessarily be nonengaging.

For the most part, students seemed engaged in these classrooms.
No matter where I went, the time when students seemed to "tune
out" was on the rare occasions when the teacher would begin to lecture. But along with this engagement and the fact that students
seemed to be much more on task in these classrooms, there was still
the nagging perception on the part of some (but not all) students that
these classes were easy. Sometimes students were surprised, actually, by the amount of work they were doing in these classes, based on
preconceived notions about these kinds of assignments. Gloria, a student from Bowness, talked about how some students assumed the
Edward Scissorhands assignment would be easy:

We thought it was going to be easy when we were watching
Edward Scissorhands, and then they gave us the assignment
[but] it wasn't. Like, we have an umbrella question for everything we do which is "How does one individual shape society's
perspectives and views?" So, to get something that deep out of
Edward Scissorhands is kind of a challenge, because it's not a
movie that's deep like that. You have to know exactly what
you're meaning. You can't b.s. at all. It doesn't work.

Angela added:

I think there's a lot more detail that goes into it than that. On the surface, it looks simple, but in reality, it's a lot more work than it is. You have to put in the same amount of thought and detail that you would into an essay, and just turn it into something visual which can be a little bit harder. Rather than writing your words, you have to show them. I think it's a lot more work than people give it credit.

Gina summarized:

There's a lot of people in the class who feel they can just get by. Like, that's everywhere, too. With *Edward Scissorhands*, you can make it deep or you can just do exactly what you have to do to get by. And so that just depends on the kind of person you are. So when they pick our groups, I hate that. 'Cause we're like workaholics. We do everything all the time. It's kind of the feeling that if you don't do it, it won't be right.

Perhaps it is just this conception that there is no right answer that leads some students to believe that new literacies classes are easy. Students are used to spending time memorizing facts to state on tests. Although students seemed to work very hard on the new literacies assignments, they weren't working to memorize things. Student engagement and involvement were certainly evident in all of these classrooms. Colin, from Parma, stated:

Actually, . . . the time just flows by. 'Cause, like on the Monument Project, every time that we would bring out the materials and start putting this together, everyone was so deeply interested in how this was going to come together that the next time you looked at the clock, it'd be time to go. Like in math class or some kind of other boring class, traditional class, you look at the clock every 3 minutes and it's not going anywhere.

In Snow Lake, student Teri said, "I've maybe had homework 10 times this year out of the whole year."
"So is that good, bad?" I asked.
"Well, it's good for us," she said, "but we're not learning as much as we should, I think. . . . We're learning more about technology and how to work the computer than like history or anything else, really."

I then asked Teri if she could remember something she did last year when she had a different teacher. "Last year, we learned a bunch of countries," she said as she laughed.

"Like what?" I asked.

"We learned facts and what the names of every state and every different . . . parts of Africa and Europe and everything."

I asked her if she could name one.

"Ohio," she answered, and then she quickly added, "No, that's not a state."

"Yes, it is," I said.

"I was thinking of Cleveland," she said. "You want me to name a state?"

In contrast, Melody, another girl in Snow Lake, felt they did not learn as much in previous years as they had with Mr. Fisher: "I thought [in previous years, it] was, like, too much homework and not enough teaching going on," she said.

Brian, also a student in Snow Lake, was exhausted by all of the technology projects he was doing, having come from a different school last year. "Too much technology bores me," he said. "It's just too much! We didn't do any in my old school. It was better. Easier."

"So you think this is harder?" I asked.

"Yeah," he responded. And Brian was one of the most intent students when he got his turn to work on his Flash ad. I observed him for many minutes as he painstakingly attempted to animate a figure entering the frame of his animation advertisement. In fact, Fisher told me that sometimes in the afternoons he reverts to typical textbook teaching, because he has noticed that students need a break from new literacies. One of his students, Chloe, confirmed this weariness: "I like technology, and I like to learn, like, new stuff about it," she said, "but sometimes he can be too pushy and push us to do this when we really don't want to. Sometimes we just want to do regular desk work and it's, 'No, we're going to the lab to learn about this that's going to happen, like, 2 million years from now.' And it's like, 'All right.'"

"And sometimes you just want to sit there, right?" I asked.

"Like in our time zone," she said, "not in, like, my grandchildren's time zone!"

Sometimes students expressed exhaustion, because they had worked hard due to the fact that they knew their work would be viewed by an external audience, most probably on the internet. Ironically, then, it may actually be the traditional manner of teaching that is "easy."

Teacher Qualities

Another entire book could be written just about the teachers' stories. Much of the data concerns their struggles. Teachers who teach new literacies seem to begin for different reasons. Some teachers (Fisher, Bernahl, and Torres) are driven by the technology. Some teachers are interested in infusing the arts into daily instruction (at Bowness and Parma). Some are more interested in social justice (Fisher and Torres). Some seem more driven by bringing out the individual capabilities and talents of their students (at Bowness and Parma). Some of the teachers have worked together in study groups to plan their instruction (at Bowness, Parma, and Peacock), while some have worked virtually alone (Rother, Fisher, and Torres). Also, an important trend that came from my data was the crucial role played in some new literacies classrooms by the school librarian (at Peacock and Bowness).

In most cases, the teachers I studied were acting out of their own personal interests in new literacies or their own intuition that this kind of teaching is best for kids. In every case, teachers' pedagogies had been informed by perhaps a single staff development presentation or some professional reading, but most all of the research and professional literature they had read was done on their own time, with little or no guidance. It could be said that these new literacies curricula and instruction are actually vernacular literacies themselves, in that these pedagogical practices have grown out of local perceived needs on the part of teachers and students. As described elsewhere (Kist, 2003), these teachers had passionate, alternative beliefs about what "counts" at school as student achievement.

In sum, the teachers studied have showed that they could change, they could collaborate, and they could persevere even when what they were doing seemed by some (and even themselves) to be failing. Rich Zasa of Parma said, "It's not 'magic time.' You have to stick to it even when it seems to be failing." Adding to their challenges, the teachers have persevered, I believe, in relative isolation—Torres spoke of the challenges he has faced and how he has tried to get the community behind him as he fought battles within his school district; at Parma High, Arts Seminar is now defunct; in Snow Lake, Fisher admitted that many of the teachers in his building are not teaching a new literacies pedagogy. While there were certainly models of teacher collaboration (Peacock and Bowness), even these collaborative groups worked in isolation from the more dominant pedagogies of their schools and districts.

CAN NEW LITERACIES BE TAUGHT IN THE CURRENT K–12 SCHOOL STRUCTURE?

There was no teacher I studied who taught in a situation in which grades did not have to be assigned. And that was really the whole point of my research: to find out how teachers were teaching new literacies in a system in which they have to assign grades. So were these teachers really creating new spaces for teaching and learning, or were they just trying to make new literacies fit into the old space? It did seem that many times there was overlap in the kids' minds—that the assignments did fulfill not only a class project goal for a grade, but that they also fulfilled some personal goal to the point that these literacy events "are part of a continual construction and negotiation of identity for people in different kinds of groups and communities" (Maybin, 2000, p. 207). In fact, this need to negotiate individual identity may not have been of paramount importance in some of the classrooms I studied, in which students continually expressed the idea that these skills would be of value to them in the workplace. Are students falling into a trap that Gee warns about, that people become essentialized into a set of skills that add value to the organization (Gee, 2000b)?

Still, some of these classrooms emphasized a search for dissonance. At Bowness High School in Calgary, for example, that was the first step of the process students followed. Harrigan stated: "You have to be good at finding ambiguity, but you have to be intrigued by it if you're a learner." At Snow Lake, Fisher explicitly discussed with his students how text positioned them. Torres and Marek at San Fernando emphasized the social responsibilities that their students have, especially now that they have all of the tools of new literacies at their disposal.

Still, I wondered if these texts (albeit "new") were fitting into the practices of people's lives rather than the other way around (Barton & Hamilton, 1998). Even though a new space was created for teaching and learning, there was still tension in that space in that teachers still had to assign some kind of grade for these projects, in order to justify time spent on them. Were these new literacies at all related to the students' own literacy practices (or should I say "events")? Were these classrooms bridging the spaces between their out-of-school and in-school literacies? Were the practices I observed those of the students or were they ultimately those of the teachers who assigned them?

The question remains: Can new literacies be taught in a traditional school environment? Fisher was helping his students create vernacular knowledge (Barton and Hamilton, 1998) with his Herb Lake project, but wasn't it still a "school project" and thus "dominant"? Can a teacher really do new literacies at school without its becoming a dominant literacy? As Barton and Hamilton wrote, "Socially powerful institutions, such as education, tend to support dominant literacy practices" (1998, p. 11). Will "new literacies," in a school environment, become just another dominant literacy practice?

What will happen to new literacies in the schools? Will something "authentic" become "nonauthentic" once it gets into schools? Is John-Steiner's (1997) "cognitive pluralism" doomed in the current structures of schools? Can a child's multiple intelligences (Gardner, 1983, 1993, 1995) ever be honored in schools? Is student motivation just something to be manipulated by the new literacies teacher in order to better teach content?

It seems that, from the beginning of recorded history, certain types of media have been coopted by the power structures of the day. Dewey (1934/1980) described how preindustrialized humans kept a "close connection of the fine arts with daily life" (p. 7). Early humans used pictorial representations to communicate, and we still have residues of this iconicity in the gestures that humans use (Danesi, 1993). Dewey lamented that as print became the dominant medium of expression and the arts became institutionalized in modern society, there was a loss of the early close relationship of the fine arts with daily life and how the arts kept humans "alive" to "sense experiences."

Of course, this legislation of expression has often accompanied the development of new forms of expression. Even the art form of sculpture was at one time controversial. For example, Michelangelo's parents didn't want him to be a sculptor, because they looked down on people who used their hands for a living (King, 2003).

Even print, which is a relatively new device of human communication (Harris, 1989; Scribner & Cole, 1981), was first the province only of the "aristocratic elite" such as the scribes of ancient Mesopotamia (Manguel, 1996). It was only the clerics' fear of the oral movement of early Christianity that resulted in the use of print to codify beliefs in the format of catechism (Resnick, 1991). The resulting focus on catechism in church settings, Resnick argued, has worked its way into our schools, with the catechism format infusing the early primers, and this influence is still strong over the format of current instruction hundreds of years later. Now, even at the start of a new millennium, with even more forms of communication available, many educators still cling to a kind of catechism, using basal readers and lower level questions that force students to spit back the "right answer." The need to measure and standardize (and thereby control) has been the educational thrust that continues to win out in our schools. Indeed, as has been pointed out, it is amazing that writing instruction currently exists in classrooms, given the challenges of measuring it (Monaghan & Saul, 1987). As Kliebard (1986) reports, the Committee of Fifteen—a group of educators from the National Education Association charged with standardizing curriculum nationally—in 1895 recommended grammar as one of the core subjects to be taught (along with reading, math, history, and geography), but not writing.

Are new literacies in danger of being forced into a kind of newtech catechism? Why are some people so afraid of the graphic-based internet? We have seen how much these crude representations coming from digital cameras from soldiers, reporters, and terrorists in the Middle East have played havoc with traditional methods of conducting war. Perhaps this accounts for the propaganda we have seen ever since the advent of television about how great it is to read print. We have slogans like Reading is Fundamental, and posters of celebrities reading books under the huge word *Read*. We continually see articles with titles such as "TV Shows That Make Your Child Want to Read."

Of course, I am heavily invested in print. As an academic, I am also locked into a very defined print medium with a very defined format. This is supposed to prove my worthiness for tenure and other academic prizes. Will the academic world catch up with the outside world that is caught up in the rising tide of sign systems? Will language arts teachers become teachers of *semiosis*—the process of emitting signs?

How will the measurers in education cope with new literacies that are multimodal, sometimes collaborative, and never static? With more forms of communication available than ever before, will educators and policymakers be able to keep a kind of catechism, with a curriculum centered around questioning that assesses students on how well they give the right answers? Or will new literacies open the way to true democratization of representational forms, maybe for the first time in history?

I reflect on all of this as I sit in Ghent, looking at St. Bavo's. Were the Van Eyck brothers trapped? Did they feel trapped back in the 1420s, forced to support the dominant state religion with their art? Or was their art a freeing thing to them? I keep thinking of the boy at Lake of Two Mountains High School who was trying to edit the raw footage into a coherent narrative. Was he trapped by new literacies? If so, was he trapped by the fact that it was an assignment or was he trapped by the conventions of traditional narrative? Or was he trapped by his own limitations? Or, rather, was he in the process of being freed to finally be able to express himself in some way, even if it was to edit together someone else's raw footage of a wedding of total strangers to him?

But my mind is beginning to cloud with all of this. Like the girl from Snow Lake, I'm beginning to feel tired of being in my "grand-children's time zone." Or maybe in this case, it's my great-great-great-great-great-grandparents' time zone, as I look around at this old city. The light is fading on the square. The pigeons flutter as a police car squeals by with the two-tone siren of Europe. Some kids are doing tricks on their bikes and cheering for each other, and some tourists sit next to me examining a map. Many people walk by with cameras and shopping bags. The bells in the tower ring, and a large group of teenagers line up and march off with some teachers, apparently on a field trip.

I look up at the church and its majesty, still existing after so many centuries and still cherished by community members and visitors from throughout the world. What of our new literacies will be left to remember 700 years from now? Will people someday go to a museum to see the display of an early website, just as they now travel to see the original Ghent altarpiece? I guess they won't have to travel, if these artifacts are digitally preserved. What will the digital museum of the future contain? What files will be treasured for centuries?

Wait, this is starting to sound familiar.

I close out this document and open a new one. I write:

INTERIOR: SCHOOL ROOM—DAY
A child of about eight sits at his desk. In the background, we hear a teacher droning about something. The child looks up, almost into the camera, sets aside his worksheet, and takes out a fresh, clean piece of paper.

New Literacy Classroom Characteristic Scale

Please answer the following items using the scale below.

5 = Very frequently
4 = Frequently
3 = Sometimes
2 = Rarely
1 = Never

_____ 1. Within the assignments I give my students, there is flexibility as to how the assignments may be completed.

_____ 2. My students work on projects that utilize more than one medium.

_____ 3. My students work on projects that require collaboration with other students.

_____ 4. My students are so engaged in their work that they lose track of time.

_____ 5. I demonstrate the uses of different media when I am working through a problem in front of the students.

_____ 6. My students draw or utilize some other form of communication when thinking through a problem or getting ready to write.

_____ 7. I talk with students about different forms of expression that are available for them to utilize.

_____ 8. My students use computers during class time.

_____ 9. My classroom features a balance of choice and mandatory activities.

_____ 10. Student work in my classroom often revolves around projects.

_____ 11. In my classroom, I am often a co-learner and a co-teacher with my students.

_____ 12. I consider myself to be a persevering teacher.

_____ 13. I consider myself to be an innovative teacher.

_____ 14. I consider myself to be a reflective teacher.

I teach at the following level (please check):
_____ K–3
_____ 4–5
_____ 6–8
_____ 9–12

I have been teaching for _____ years.

REFERENCES

Alexander-Smith, A.C. (2004). Feeling the rhythm of the critically conscious mind. *English Journal, 93*(3), 58–63.

Allen, W. (Director). (1979). *Manhattan* [Motion Picture]. United States: United Artists.

Alvermann, D.E. (2002). Preface. In D.E. Alvermann (Ed.), *Adolescents and literacies in a digital world* (pp. vii–xi). New York: Peter Lang.

Alvermann, D.E., & Hagood, M.C. (2000). Fandom and critical media literacy. *Journal of Adolescent & Adult Literacy, 43*, 436–446.

Alvermann, D.E. & Heron, A.H. (2001). Literacy identity work: Playing to learn with popular media. *Journal of Adolescent & Adult Literacy, 45*, 118–122.

Alvermann, D.E., Moon, J.S., & Hagood, M.C. (1999). *Popular culture in the classroom: Teaching and researching critical media literacy.* Newark, DE: International Reading Association.

Avila, C. (Director). (2000). *The price of glory* [Motion Picture]. United States: New Line Cinema.

Barton, D., & Hamilton, M. (1998). *Local literacies: Reading and writing in one community.* London: Routledge.

Bean, T.W., & Moni, K. (2003). Developing students' critical literacy: Exploring identity construction in young adult fiction. *Journal of Adolescent & Adult Literacy, 46*, 638–648.

Beavis, C., & Nixon, H. (2003, September). *Places of gathering: Space and community in multiplayer computer games.* Multiliteracies: The Contact Zone. Paper presented at the meeting of the Association Internationale de Linguistique Appliquée (AILA), Ghent, Belgium.

Berkeley, B. (Director). (1941). *Babes on Broadway* [Motion Picture]. United States: Metro-Goldwyn-Mayer.

Blackburn, M.V. (2003). Disrupting the (hetero)normative: Exploring literacy performances and identity work with queer youth. *Journal of Adolescent & Adult Literacy, 46*, 312–324.

Blasé, D.W. (2000). A new sort of writing: E-mail in the E-nglish classroom. *English Journal, 90*(2), 47–51.

Bloome, D., & Egan-Robertson, A. (1993). The social construction of intertextuality and classroom reading and writing. *Reading Research Quarterly, 28*(4), 303–333.

Bogdanovich, P. (Interviewer). (1997). *Who the devil made it? Conversations with Robert Aldrich et al.* New York: Knopf.

Brown, J. S., Collins, A., & Duguid, P. (1989). Situated cognition and the culture of learning. *Educational Researcher, 18*(1), 32–42.

Brownlow, K. (1968). *The parade's gone by.* New York: Ballantine.

Bruce, B.C. (2002). Diversity and critical social engagement: How changing technologies enable new modes of literacy in changing circumstances. In D.E. Alvermann (Ed.), *Adolescents and literacies in a digital world* (pp. 1–18). New York: Peter Lang.

Bruce, B.C., & Bishop, A.P. (2002). Using the web to support inquiry-based literacy development. *Journal of Adolescent & Adult Literacy, 45,* 706–714.

Buckingham, D. (1993). *Reading audiences: Young people and the media.* Manchester, England: Manchester University Press.

Buckingham, D. (2003). *Media education: Literacy, learning and contemporary culture.* Cambridge, UK: Polity Press.

Buckingham, D., & Sefton-Green, J. (1994). *Cultural studies goes to school: Reading and teaching popular media.* London: Taylor & Francis.

Burton, T. (Director). (1990). *Edward Scissorhands* [Motion Picture]. United States: Twentieth Century Fox.

Bustle, L.S. (2004). The role of visual representation in the assessment of learning. *Journal of Adolescent & Adult Literacy, 47,* 416–423.

Callahan, M., & Low, B.E. (2004). At the crossroads of expertise: The risky business of teaching popular culture. *English Journal, 93*(3), 52–57.

Chandler-Olcott, K., & Mahar, D. (2003a). Adolescents' anime-inspired "fanfictions": An exploration of multiliteracies. *Journal of Adolescent & Adult Literacy, 46,* 556–566.

Chandler-Olcott, K., & Mahar, D. (2003b). "Tech-savviness" meets multiliteracies: Exploring adolescent girls' technology-mediated literacy practices. *Reading Research Quarterly, 38,* 356–385.

Chaplin, C. (Director). (1921). *The kid* [Motion Picture]. United States: First National Pictures.

Cohn, M. (Director). (1997). *Snow White: Tale of terror* [Motion Picture]. United States: Interscope/PolyGram.

Coiro, J. (2003). Reading comprehension on the internet: Expanding our understanding of reading comprehension to encompass new literacies. *The Reading Teacher, 56,* 458–464.

Commission on Adolescent Literacy. (1999). *Adolescent literacy: A position statement.* Newark, DE: International Reading Association.

Cope, B., & Kalantzis, M., for the New London Group. (Eds.). (2000). *Multiliteracies: Literacy learning and the design of social futures.* London: Routledge.

Costanzo, W.V. (1992). *Reading the movies: Twelve great films on video and how to teach them.* Urbana, IL: National Council of Teachers of English.

Csikszentmihalyi, M. (1990). *Flow: The psychology of optimal experience.* New York: HarperCollins.

Csikszentmihalyi, M. (1991). Literacy and intrinsic motivation. In S. R.

Graubard (Ed.), *Literacy: An overview by fourteen experts* (pp. 115–140). New York: Hill & Wang.

Csikszentmihalyi, M. (1993). *The evolving self: A psychology for the third millennium.* New York: HarperCollins.

Danesi, M. (1993). *Messages and meanings: An introduction to semiotics.* Toronto: Canadian Scholars' Press.

Darabont, F. (Director). (1994). *The Shawshank redemption* [Motion Picture]. United States: Columbia.

Delpit, L. (1995). *Other people's children: Cultural conflict in the classroom.* New York: New Press.

Dewey, J. (1980). *Art as experience.* New York: Perigee Books. (Original work published 1934)

Dewey, J. (1990). *The school and society.* Chicago: University of Chicago Press. (Original work published 1902)

Dick, E. (1991). *From limelight to satellite: A Scottish film book.* London: British Film Institute.

Doherty, C., & Mayer, D. (2003). E-mail as a "contact zone" for teacher-student relationships. *Journal of Adolescent & Adult Literacy, 46,* 592–600.

Dreher, P. (2000). Electronic poetry: Student-constructed hypermedia. *English Journal, 90*(2), 68–73.

Duncan, H. (1984). *Kate Rice: Prospector.* Toronto: Simon & Pierre.

Edwards, B. (1987). *Drawing on the artist within.* New York: Fireside.

Edwards, B. (1989). *Drawing on the right side of the brain.* New York: J.P. Tarcher.

Eisner, E. (1992). The misunderstood role of the arts in human development. *Phi Delta Kappan, 73,* 591–595.

Eisner, E. (1994). *Cognition and curriculum reconsidered* (2nd ed.). New York: Teachers College Press.

Eisner, E. (1997). Cognition and representation: A way to pursue the American dream? *Phi Delta Kappan, 78,* 349–353.

Eisner, E. (2002). *The arts and the creation of mind.* New Haven, CT: Yale University Press.

Evans, J. (2004). From Sheryl Crow to Homer Simpson: Literature and composition through pop culture. *English Journal, 93*(3), 32–38.

Fairclough, N. (1989). *Language and power.* London: Longman.

Fairclough, N. (1995). *Critical discourse analysis: The critical study of language.* New York: Longman.

Fischman, G.E. (2001). Reflections about images, visual, culture, and educational research. *Educational Researcher, 30*(8), 28–33.

Foster, H. M. (2002). *Crossing over: Teaching meaning-centered secondary English language arts* (2nd ed.). Mahwah, NJ: Erlbaum.

Freebody, P., & Luke, A. (1990). "Literacies" programs: Debates and demands in cultural context. *Prospect, 5,* 7–16.

Freire, P. (1970). *Pedagogy of the oppressed.* New York: Continuum.

Frey, N., & Fisher, D. (2004). Using graphic novels, anime, and the internet in an urban high school. *English Journal, 93*(3), 19–25.

Gardner, H. (1983). *Frames of mind: The theory of multiple intelligences.* New York: Basic Books.

Gardner, H. (1993). *Multiple intelligences: The theory into practice.* New York: Basic Books.

Gardner, H. (1995). Reflections on multiple intelligences. *Phi Delta Kappan, 76,* 200–209.

Garner, J.F. (1995). *Politically correct bedtime stories: Modern tales for our life and times.* New York: Macmillan.

Gee, J. P. (1996). *Social linguistics and literacies: Ideology in discourses* (2nd ed.). London: Falmer Press.

Gee, J.P. (2000a). The new literacy studies: From "socially situated" to the work of the social. In D. Barton, M. Hamilton, & R. Ivanic (Eds.), *Situated literacies: Reading and writing in context* (pp. 180–196). London: Routledge.

Gee, J.P. (2000b). New people in new worlds: networks, the new capitalism and schools. In B. Cope & M. Kalantzis, for the New London Group (Eds.), *Multiliteracies: Literacy learning and the design of social futures* (pp. 43–68). London: Routledge.

Gee, J.P. (2002). Millennials and bobos, Blue's Clues and Sesame Street: A story for our times. In D.E. Alvermann (Ed.), *Adolescents and literacies in a digital world* (pp. 51–67). New York: Peter Lang.

Gee, J. P. (2003). *What video games have to teach us about learning and literacy.* New York: Palgrave Macmillan.

Giannetti, L. (2001). *Understanding movies* (9th ed.). Upper Saddle River, NJ: Prentice-Hall.

Glaser, B.G., & Strauss, A.L. (1967). *The discovery of grounded theory.* Chicago: Aldine.

Gombrich, E.H. (1960). *Art and illusion: A study in the psychology of pictorial representation.* Princeton, NJ: Princeton University Press.

Gordimer, N. (1956). Happy Event. In *Six feet of the country: Fifteen short stories.* London: Penguin.

Green, B. (1988). Subject-specific literacy and school learning: A focus on writing. *Australian Journal of Education, 32,* 156–179.

Greene, M. (1997). Metaphors and multiples: Representation, the arts, and history. *Phi Delta Kappan, 78,* 387–394.

Greeno, J. G., & Hall, R. P. (1997). Practicing representation: Learning with and about representational forms. *Phi Delta Kappan, 78,* 361–367.

Greer, W.D. (1997). *Art as a basic: The reformation in art education.* Bloomington, IN: Phi Delta Kappa.

Hagood, M. (2003). New media and online literacies: No age left behind. *Reading Research Quarterly, 38,* 387–391.

Hand, D. (Director). (1937). *Snow White and the seven dwarfs* [Motion Picture]. United States: Disney.

Harris, W.V. (1989). *Anicent literacy.* Cambridge, MA: Harvard University Press.

Hawisher, G. (2000). Constructing our identities through online images. *Journal of Adolescent & Adult Literacy, 43,* 544–552.

Heath, S.B. (2001). Three's not a crowd: Plans, roles, and focus in the arts. *Educational Researcher, 30*(7), 10–17.

Hibbing, A.N., & Rankin-Erickson, J.L. (2003). A picture is worth a thousand words. Using visual images to improve comprehension for middle school struggling readers. *The Reading Teacher, 56,* 758–770.

Hitchcock, A. (Director). (1959). *North by northwest* [Motion Picture]. United States: Metro-Goldwyn–Mayer.

Hitchcock, A. (Director). (1960). *Psycho* [Motion Picture]. United States: Shamley Productions.

Hobbs, R., & Frost, R. (2003). Measuring the acquisition of media-literacy skills. *Reading Research Quarterly, 38,* 330–355.

John-Steiner, V. (1997). *Notebooks of the mind: Explorations of thinking* (Rev. ed.). New York: Oxford University Press.

Kerr, W. (1975). *The silent clowns.* New York: Knopf.

King, R. (2003). *Michelangelo and the pope's ceiling.* New York: Walker & Co.

Kist, W. (2000). Beginning to create the new literacy classroom: What does the new literacy look like? *Journal of Adolescent & Adult Literacy, 43,* 710–718.

Kist, W. (2002). Finding "new literacy" in action: An interdisciplinary high school Western civilization class. *Journal of Adolescent & Adult Literacy, 45,* 368–377.

Kist, W. (2003). Student achievement in new literacies for the twenty-first century. *Middle School Journal, 35*(1), 6–13. Also online at http://www.nmsa.org/services/msj/msj_september2003.htm#a

Klein, N. (2000). *No logo: Taking aim at the brand bullies.* New York: Picador.

Kliebard, H. M. (1986). *The struggle for the American curriculum 1893–1958.* New York: Routledge.

Kress, G. (1997). *Before writing: Rethinking the paths to literacy.* London: Routledge.

Kress, G. (2003). *Literacy in the new media age.* London: Routledge.

Lankshear, C. (with Gee, J. P., Knobel, M., & Searle, C.) (1997). *Changing literacies.*Buckingham, England: Open University Press.

Lankshear, C., & Knobel, M. (2003). *New literacies: Changing knowledge and classroom learning.* Buckingham: Open University Press.

Leander, K. (2003). Writing travelers' tales on new literacyscapes. *Reading Research Quarterly, 38,* 392–397.

Lee, G. (2003). Kamishibai: A vehicle to multiple literacies. *Voices from the Middle, 10*(3), 36–42.

Leland, C. H., & Harste, J. C. (1994). Multiple ways of knowing: Curriculum in a new key. *Language Arts, 71,* 337–345.

Lemke, J.L. (2003, December). *Towards critical multimedia literacy.*

Paper presented at the meeting of the National Reading Conference (NRC), Scottsdale, AZ. Retrieved April 29, 2004 at: www-personal.umich.edu/~jaylemke/webs/nrc_2003.htm

Lemke, J.L. (2004, April). Learning across multiple places and their chronotopes. Paper presented at the meeting of the American Educational Research Association (AERA), San Diego, CA. Retrieved April 29, 2004, from: http://www.personal.umich.edu/~jaylemke/papers/aera_2004.htm

Leu, D.J., Jr. (1996). Sarah's secret: Social aspects of literacy and learning in a digital information age. *The Reading Teacher, 50,* 162–165.

Leu, D.J., Jr. (1997). Caity's question: Literacy as deixis on the Internet. *The Reading Teacher, 51,* 62–67.

Leu, D.J., Jr. (2001). Internet project: Preparing students for new literacies in a global village. *The Reading Teacher, 54,* 568–572.

Leu, D.J., Jr. (2002). Internet workshop: Making time for literacy. *The Reading Teacher, 55,* 466–472.

Levin, B., & Wiens, J. (2003). There is another way: A different approach to education reform. *Phi Delta Kappan, 84,* 658–664.

Luke, A. (2000). Critical literacy in Australia: A matter of context and standpoint. *Journal of Adult & Adolescent Literacy, 43,* 448–461.

Luke, C. (2000). New literacies in teacher education. *Journal of Adult & Adolescent Literacy, 43,* 424–435.

Luke, C. (2003). Pedagogy, connectivity, multimodality, and interdisciplinarity. *Reading Research Quarterly, 38,* 397–403.

Lusted, D. (Ed.). (1991). *The media studies book: A guide for teachers.* London: Routledge.

Maness, K. (2004). Teaching media-savvy students about the popular media. *English Journal, 93*(3), 46–51.

Manguel, A. (1996). *A history of reading.* New York: Viking.

Masterman, L. (1986). *Teaching the media.* London: Marion Boyars.

Maybin, J. (2000). The new literacy studies: context, intertextuality and discourse. In D. Barton, M. Hamilton, & R. Ivanic (Eds.), *Situated literacies: Reading and writing in context* (pp. 197–209). London: Routledge.

McGuire, R. (1995). Moon over Parma. [Recorded by D. Carey]. On *Cleveland Rocks!: Music from the Drew Carey Show* [CD]. Los Angeles, CA: Rhino Records.

McLaren, P. (1989). *Life in schools: An introduction to critical pedagogy in the foundations of education.* New York: Longman.

Merriam, S. B. (1998). *Qualitative research and case study applications in education.* San Francisco: Jossey-Bass.

Messaris, P. (1994). *Visual literacy: Image, mind and reality.* Boulder, CO: Westview Press.

Metz, C. (1974). *Film language: A semiotics of the cinema.* (Michael Taylor, Trans.). New York: Oxford University Press.

Moje, E.B., Young, J.P., Readence, J.E., & Moore, D.W. (2000). Reinventing adolescent literacy for new times: perennial and millennial issues.

Journal of Adolescent & Adult Literacy 43, 400–410.

Monaco, J. (2000). *How to read a film: The world of movies, media, and multimedia.* New York: Oxford University Press.

Monaghan, E. J., & Saul, E. W. (1987). The reader, the scribe, the thinker: A critical look at the history of American reading and writing instruction. In T. S. Popkewitz (Ed.), *The formation of the school subjects: The struggle for creating an American institution* (pp. 85–122). Philadelphia, PA: Falmer.

Morrell, E. (2002). Toward a critical pedagogy of popular culture: Literacy development among urban youth. *Journal of Adolescent & Adult Literacy, 46,* 72–77.

Morrison, T.G., Bryan, G., & Chilcoat, G.W. (2002). Using student-generated comic books in the classroom. *Journal of Adolescent & Adult Literacy, 45,* 758–767.

National Council of Teachers of English & International Reading Association. (1996). *Standards for the English language arts.* Newark, DE & Urbana, IL: National Council of Teachers of English & International Reading Association.

New London Group. (1996). A pedagogy of multiliteracies: Designing social futures. *Harvard Educational Review, 66*(1), 60–92.

Nixon, H. (2003). New research literacies for contemporary research into literacy and new media? *Reading Research Quarterly, 38,* 407–413.

Norton, B. (2003). The motivating power of comic books: Insights from Archie comic readers. *The Reading Teacher, 57,* 140–147.

Patterson, N. G. (2000). Hypertext and the changing roles of readers. *English Journal, 90*(2), 74–80.

Paul, D.G. (2000). Rap and orality: Critical media literacy, pedagogy, and cultural synchronization. *Journal of Adolescent & Adult Literacy, 44,* 246–251.

Reinking, D. (1995). Reading and writing with computers: Literacy research in a post-typographic world. In K.A. Hinchman, D.J. Leu, & C.K. Kinzer (Eds.), *Yearbook of the National Reading Conference, No. 44: Perspectives on literacy research and practice* (pp. 17–33). Chicago: National Reading Conference.

Reinking, D. (1997). Me and my hypertext:) A multiple digression analysis of technology and literacy (sic). *The Reading Teacher, 50,* 626–643.

Resnick, D. P. (1991). Historical perspectives on literacy and schooling. In S. R. Graubard (Ed.), *Literacy: An overview by fourteen experts* (pp. 15–32). New York: Hill & Wang.

Riel, M., & Fulton, K. (2001). The role of technology in supporting learning communities. *Phi Delta Kappan, 82,* 518–523.

Rogers, R. (2002). "That's what you're here for, you're suppose to tell us": Teaching and learning critical literacy. *Journal of Adolescent & Adult Literacy, 45,* 772–787.

Romano, T. (1995). *Writing with passion: Life stories, multiple genres.*

Portsmouth, NH: Boynton/Cook.

Romano, T. (2000). *Blending genre, altering style: Writing multigenre papers.* Portsmouth, NH: Boynton/Cook.

Rother, L. (2000). *The impact of a media literacy curriculum on the literate behavior of at-risk adolescents.* Unpublished doctoral dissertation. McGill University, Quebec, Canada.

Rother, L. (2002). Media literacy and at-risk students: A Canadian perspective. *Telemedium, 48*(2), 13–16.

Schmar-Dobler, E. (2003). Reading on the internet: The link between literacy and technology. *Journal of Adolescent & Adult Literacy, 47,* 80–85.

Schmidt, P. (2001). *The Ghent altarpiece.* Ghent, Belgium: Ludion.

Scribner, S., & Cole, M. (1981). *The psychology of literacy.* Cambridge, MA: Harvard University Press.

Shafer, G. (2000). Prime time literature in the high school. *English Journal, 90*(2), 93–96.

Short, K., & Harste, J. (with Burke, C.). (1996). *Creating classrooms for authors and inquirers* (2nd ed.). Portsmouth, NH: Heinemann.

Short, K., Kauffman, G., & Kahn, L. (2000). "I just need to draw": Responding to literature across multiple sign systems. *The Reading Teacher, 54,* 160–171.

Sipe, R.B. (2000). Virtually being there: Creating authentic experiences through interactive exchanges. *English Journal, 90*(2), 104–111.

Soja, E.W. (1989). *Postmodern geographies: The reassertion of space in critical social theory.* London: Verso

Soja, E.W. (1996). *Thirdspace: Journeys to Los Angeles and other real and imagined places.* Cambridge, MA: Blackwell.

Street, B. (1995). *Social literacies: Critical approaches to literacy in development, ethnography and education.* New York: Longman.

Street, B. (2003, September). *Theory and practice of literacy under challenge: Some responses.* Multiliteracies: The Contact Zone. Paper presented at the meeting of the Association Internationale de Linguistique Appliquée (AILA), Ghent, Belgium.

Tishman, S., & Perkins, D. (1997). The language of thinking. *Phi Delta Kappan, 78,* 368–374.

Tornatore, G. (Director). (1989). *Cinema paradiso* [Motion Picture]. Italy: Cristaldifilm

Tsurusaki, B.K., Deaton, B.E., Hay, K.E., & Thomson, N. (2003). *Virtual gorilla modeling project: Knowledge-in-the-making through the cascade of models.* Paper presented at the meeting of the American Educational Research Association, Chicago, IL.

Tyner, K. (1998). *Literacy in a digital world: Teaching and learning in the age of information.* Mahwah, NJ: Erlbaum.

Valdez, L. (Director). (1987). *La bamba* [Motion Picture]. United States: Columbia.

Van Wyhe, T.L.C. (2000). A passion for poetry: Breaking rules and boundaries with online relationships. *English Journal, 90*(2), 60–67.

Versaci, R. (2001). How comic books can change the way our students see literature: One teacher's perspective. *English Journal, 91*(2), 61–67.

Vetrie, M. (2004). Using film to increase literacy skills. *English Journal, 93*(3), 39–45.

Vygotsky, L. S. (1978). *Mind in society: The development of higher psychological processes.* Cambridge, MA: Harvard University Press.

Vygotsky, L.S. (1986). *Thought and language.* Cambridge, MA: MIT Press. (Original work published 1934)

Walling, D.R. (2001). Rethinking visual arts education: A convergence of influences. *Phi Delta Kappan, 82,* 626–631.

Wallowitz, L. (2004). Reading as resistance: Gendered messages in literature and media. *English Journal, 93*(3), 26–31.

Weir, P. (Director). (1986). *The Mosquito Coast* [Motion Picture]. United States: Warner Brothers.

Whitin, P. (2002). Leading into literature circles through the sketch-to-stretch strategy. *The Reading Teacher, 55,* 444–450.

Williams, B. (2003). What they see is what we get: Television and middle school writers. *Journal of Adolescent & Adult Literacy, 46*(7), 546–554.

Willinsky, J. (1990). *The new literacy: Redefining reading and writing in the schools.* New York: Routledge.

Wood, G. (1992). *Schools that work.* New York: Dutton.

Young, J.P., Dillon, D.R., & Moje, E.B. (2002). Shape-shifting portfolios: Millennial youth, literacies, and the game of life. In D.E. Alvermann (Ed.), *Adolescents and literacies in a digital world* (pp. 114–131). New York: Peter Lang.

Zwick, E. (Director). (1998). *The siege* [Motion Picture]. United States: Twentieth Century Fox.

INDEX

ABOUT THE AUTHOR

William Kist is an assistant professor at Kent State University–Stark Campus, where he teaches literacy methods courses for pre-service teachers. He has been a middle school and high school language arts teacher for the Akron Public Schools; a language arts and social studies curriculum coordinator for the Medina County Schools' Educational Service Center and the Hudson City Schools; and a consultant and trainer for school districts across the United States. Kist has over 30 national and international conference presentations and 10 published articles to his credit.

In addition to his work in education, Kist has worked as a video producer and musician. He is the recipient of an Ohio Educational Broadcasting Network Commission (OEBIE) Honorable Mention and a regional Emmy Award nomination for outstanding achievement in music composition. Kist is developing his original screenplay, *Field Trip*, to be filmed as an independent feature in 2006.